Journey Management

Unleashing the Strategic Power of Change

Journey Management
Unleashing the Strategic Power of Change

Jimmy Brown, Ph.D.

Jill Royston

Journey Management
Unleashing the Strategic Power of Change

ISBN-13: 978-0615806297 (sc)
ISBN-10: 0615806295

Printed in the United States of America

Contents

Acknowledgments

The authors would like to acknowledge the gracious support of the Beacon Associates leadership team who helped us bring this vision to reality. In particular we would like to thank Mr. Mason Holloway, who has graciously allowed us to leverage parts of his Performance DNA™ methodology into this approach. We would also like to acknowledge Elly Zupko, who was invaluable in helping us produce a quality text. It is a honor to be able to work with such wonderful people.

Introduction

There is nothing more constant in business than change. Truth be told, however, there are also few things that create more fear and dread. Send out an e-mail announcing an upcoming change, and the grumbles of discord could be deafening. Those grumbles are likely to be followed by resistance and disruption that could derail the whole effort. It doesn't matter whether it is *blind resistance, political resistance,* or *ideological resistance* (Burke, 2002), individuals' antipathy towards a shift in their workplace is often the number one driver that inhibits a change effort from reaching its stated goals, and prevents you from achieving your business goals.

Even when the resistance is minimal, there may be other factors both inside and outside of the organization that can cause problems. Poor planning, lack of coordination, even just plain old bad luck can quickly get in the way of value realization. The irony of all this is that, while there is no question that organizational change is extremely challenging, research and experience both show that the ability to effectively change in relation to market conditions is a major differentiator between high performing organizations and their competition (Schein, 2003; Worley, Hitchin, & Ross, 1996). If we recognize this as true, we must then ask how do we harness the power of change to drive this peak performance?

The first step is recognizing that no organization ever has just one change. They all have multiple changes throughout their lifecycle. We must also recognize that most people have already been through some organizational changes in their work life. While some of those experiences may have been positive, there is a high probability that nearly every person has been through at least one change that they do not recall fondly. For better or worse, those are the experiences they are likely to key in on. Given all this, we must begin every change effort by accepting that personal and organizational histories that are completely unrelated to our efforts may be competing with our efforts. This is not anything we can't handle, simply a fact of organizational life.

Another important recognition is that there are almost always multiple changes happening at the same time. Sure, there might be very small businesses (e.g., a three-person insurance office) where there is only one change at a time. Any corporation of reasonable size, however, is likely to have multiple changes at once. Some changes may be big, while others may be small. Some may start at different times while others impact multiple departments. The important thing to remember is that it is never just one change and it is never just one change at a time. All the changes are interconnected parts of an organization's evolution. As such, we must manage not just individual changes, but the entire change journey. Managing that journey is the focus of this book.

The Types of Change

There are two things about change we need to accept. The first is that change is hard and also unavoidable. The unavoidability of change leads to the second thing we need to accept, which is that the ability to effectively manage change is one of the most important strategic advantages an organization can have (Worley, Hitchin, & Ross, 1996). Accepting these two things as true leads to the all important question of *how do we go about leveraging our ability to change as a strategic advantage*? The answer depends on a number of factors. These factors could include timing, history, external drivers, and even what we'll politely term the attention of senior executives (or more importantly the occasional lack thereof). One of the most important factors that impact how we manage a change is what kind of change is happening. While there are a number of different options for categorizing change, we will do so by putting changes into one of three buckets: Tactical, Strategic, or Evolutionary.

Tactical changes are usually finite in scope and confined to a single department or division. This category includes simple changes, such as implementing some new accounting system or modifying a production process. Technically, they may include things as mundane as moving the team from one floor to another, or the assignment of a new supervisor. While those changes can also be challenging, the focus of this book is how people do their work, not so much where or for whom. As such, we're not too worried about changes that are solely a function of personnel shifts.

While Tactical changes do have challenges as far as retraining and developing buy-in, the limited impact usually makes them more manageable. Often the people who must adopt the change and the people impacted by the change are the same people. Unlike some large changes, the limited impact means we often see these two groups interact face-to-face, or at least via the phone in real time. This allows questions to be answered more specifically and directly, rather than having to guess at their questions and respond through things like Frequently Asked Question (FAQ) lists or in mass communications. There is still likely to be lots of grumbling by the impacted individuals, but it is rare for someone to decide to leave an organization over a tactical change.

A Strategic change is at least division-wide, if not across an entire organization. The explicit or implicit goal is to bring some new value to the organizational entity. It is important to note that the use of the term "value" here refers to some kind of *increase in measureable benefit to the company*. The benefit may be assessed along metrics such as increasing return-on-investment, increasing share of customer wallet, or even brand expansion into a new market or vertical. The term should not to be confused with ethical or moral standards of the organization, which are also sometimes termed as "values." While this second category of values is important, and can drive decisions around the first category, the focus of Strategic change is on impacting the measurable business value.

Strategic changes often occur when an organization merges with (or is acquired by) another organization, or new leadership comes in and shifts the direction of the organization. Strategic changes always have multiple operational impacts that could each be considered a Tactical change. The cultural impacts, however, are the greatest concern. The cultural impacts of change are often underestimated, and rarely well managed. Not surprisingly, these are the kind of changes that individuals tend to be most resistant to because they feel the effects on their relationships at work, their ways of working, and/or their roles. This resistance can vary from loud objection, to social loafing, to sabotaging the change activities. Some people even choose to leave the organization. Careful attention and active administration of strategic change—particularly the cultural impacts—will help the organization achieve the intended business benefits.

There are several common challenges that can prevent organizations from properly managing Strategic changes and the many Tactical changes within them. The most common challenge is the organization's collective unwillingness to challenge current business practices, processes, and systems and admit that what got us here won't get us there. As we will discuss in the next chapter, this resistance to change tends to take on three distinct forms that needs to be managed in specific ways.

Evolutionary change, sometime called revolutionary change when fast paced, occurs when an entire organization or industry changes due to some variation in the business ecosystem. Interestingly, the organization itself is often more resistant to these types of changes than the individual people because evolutionary change requires challenging the business practices, processes, and systems that created the current success. For example, Digital Equipment Corporation (DEC) was very resistant to the change from mainframes to PCs and was unwilling to evolve (Schein, 2003). As a result, DEC no longer exists today. Many other organizations are resisting the progression from PCs to cloud and risk suffering a similar fate. To deal with this kind of change an organization must be willing to commit to and manage a Strategic change that responds to these new needs, as well as the many Tactical changes within that.

For all types of change, we must recognize that the current practices represent three things to people working in an organization: commitment to a collective future, method to be successful (individually and organizationally), and confidence in past decisions.

All the choices we have made in an organization, even the compromises and less-than-stellar decisions, were made based on a shared commitment to a collective future. Evolutionary or Strategic changes are more likely to stir doubt and force people to question the commitment to a collective future. Leaders recommend Strategic and Evolutionary changes based on their view of the marketplace or eco-system and their assumptions about what will help the business grow. Employees don't have the same information or assumptions that the leaders have, and when this "new" future is described it may not make sense or seem necessary. At this point, employees are no longer sure if the leaders' decisions support the best possible for the organization and the employees.

Even tactical changes, like relocating HR Partners from sitting with clients to sitting with functional HR teams, call into question the shared picture we were committed to before. However, it is easier for people to get the information they need to understand how tactical changes support the collective future. Information and influence are the keys to helping people understand the "new" collective future and to help them move past their concerns about letting go of their current view.

Current methods are usually the most preferred, even more so when they have been successful. The current ways of working (politics, structure, processes) are known to people. Even if it is a broken, dysfunctional, or ineffective way of working, people know how to work it to be successful. Think about it: any success a person has had to date—from the V.P. of Sales who just received a huge bonus for exceeding goals, to the Production Manager who just became employee of the month—was created using the existing practices, structure, and processes. When we introduce any change, whether it is Tactical, Strategic, Evolutionary, we are essentially saying "stop doing the thing that has brought you success and try this!" We force people to let go of what has worked so far on the belief that different will be better. In order to move people away from current practices and commit to the change you are expecting, they have to believe the new way of working will lead to success for them. If they don't see a good outcome or path to success—*for them*—they are unlikely to commit. We will discuss this more when we talk about enabling key influencers and overcoming resistance to change.

The biggest roadblock to Strategic and Evolutionary change is that people have (or at least they must appear to have) confidence in their past decisions. Entertaining the possibility (or scoping the reality) of a Strategic or Evolutionary change requires people to consider that their past/current choices may not help their business progress. Most leaders are incentivized, rewarded, and expected to "know" which way to go and to convince others that they are right about their choices. When leaders or employees are confronted with information about a changing marketplace, eco-system, or even new business practice, they will initially cling to their current approach because it was a "good" decision at the time and because it was what they were hired to do.

Regardless of the type of change, current practices—and what they represent to the organization—are a compelling pull toward the status quo. This challenge is usually overcome when the organization is faced with some significant disruption driver such as a significant drop in profit, critical Wall Street or stakeholder pressure, or a mass exodus of top talent, which forces an organization to "change or die" (Deutschman, 2005). This is not unlike the idea from *The Seven Habits of Highly Effective People* that, for an individual to change, their "yes" must be stronger than their "no" (Covey, 2004). Only this time, that "yes" has to be stronger for a large group of people—not just one.

The next challenge to effectively initiate and manage both Strategic and Evolutionary changes is a leader's inability to perceive the interconnections that are causing shifts in their business ecosystem and within their organization. A lack of "systems thinking" at executive levels will not only prevent leaders from anticipating the need for Strategic change, but will also keep their focus on the many individual Tactical changes without ever linking them together to create meaningful business outcomes. This challenge typically gets addressed in one of two ways. The first way is that a new leader with a different perspective (e.g., an organizational systems view) takes over and leads from an expanded vision. The second way this challenge can be addressed is when an existing leader recognizes that the current approaches are simply no longer working. While this is very difficult to influence, it is much easier to influence than developing a new leader. We find that taking a data-driven approach to these efforts tends to be the most effective.

The last challenge we want to discuss is the lack of tools to effectively manage Strategic change and the related Tactical changes. Typical approaches—the practices that helped people be successful so far—are linear and easy-to-follow. Some organizations have the tools to manage several projects into a program, but how many do you know that can effectively manage several programs into a Strategic business shift that causes differentiated value in the market? Even if an organization sees the need to manage Strategic change and builds the systems thinking capability to manage it, they may be stopped in their tracks by ineffective or unavailable tools.

We have introduced three kinds of change; while each has different drivers and dynamics, they are all interrelated and that interrelatedness must be managed. This is a novel concept to many organizations as the legacy of scientific management is to break things down into their component parts. This is a great approach as long as we remember to reassemble those parts to understand how they interact as a whole. In this case, reassembly means accepting that there is not one change, or even lots of individual changes, but a single journey with many parts that must be actively managed to unleash the strategic value of the organization. This understanding—that we are managing not just change but a *journey* —will guide the rest of our discussion.

Change is Hard and People Don't Like It . . .

Yes, the title of this chapter is very blunt. But it is also accurate. For those experienced with managing change, this information is likely to elicit the kind of sarcastic response that indicates they already knew this. For those new to managing change, this insight may not be a surprise, but the depth of the challenge may not have full sunk in yet. Regardless of where one stands on this awareness continuum, we have to be honest about how change is perceived in our organizations.

When we announce that a change is coming, we are likely to hear comments like:

- "This whole thing will be nothing but a distraction."
- "We don't need or want this."
- "We won't be able to do our jobs effectively with all this going on."

While the volume and tone of these comments may vary depending on the scope and impact of the change, we have to be ready for the fact that some people are not going to be excited about the shifts. Moreover, some people are going to predict that the particular change will fail. A few may even prophesy that the change will be the downfall of the organization, and the world as we know it. The irony of these doom and gloom predictions is that the only way to avoid an organizational apocalypse is being able to adapt and change with the ever-evolving business world (Worley, Hitchin, & Ross, 1996). If you want to succeed, you have to be able to evolve and adapt with the market. In other words, effectively manage change. To effectively do that we have to be willing to accept that it isn't easy and be willing to do the hard work to make it as effective as possible.

This is often the point where people ask why change is so hard? To illustrate why, let's imagine we have one person trying to change their eating habits to be healthier. Doing so takes discipline, dedication, and drive. They are likely to have fits and starts along the way, and not to be able to fully change without falling back into their old habits several times. To effectively change, they have to be convinced that the benefits of change are equal to or greater than the effort required to make the change (Covey, 2004). Most importantly, they need to have a plan, and be ready to stick to that plan until the change becomes permanent. Even under the best of circumstances it may take this person several months to fully adjust what they choose to eat or not eat.

Now let's imagine that we have two people trying to change the way they interact with each other. It becomes at least twice as hard. So what happens when we look at a group of 100, 1000, or more than 10,000 people? It's pretty easy to guess how much more difficult it will be for that many people to choose to do things differently. Add in multiple changes at once and the difficulty increases by orders of magnitude. This is the reason why managing change is so important in our organizations. Despite the recognition that this is a difficult process, some organizations seem to keep trying to convince people that the change won't be that bad and not to worry about investing the time and resources into managing it. For the record, we have never once seen this approach work.

If people have been with an organization for any length of time, they are likely to be at least content with the way things are. If they were overly discontent, they probably would have left at their first opportunity. As a result, any announcement that a change is coming will generate some degree of fear and anxiety. Ignoring those issues won't make them go away, and trying to spin the story to make the change seem like "no big deal" will not work on anyone but the most gullible. The rest of the people in the organization are likely to resist the change in a variety of ways. This resistance comes in three primary flavors: blind resistance, political resistance, and ideological resistance (Burke, 2002). Each flavor has its own characteristics and should be dealt with in its own way.

Blind resistance is the simplest. It is where someone doesn't like change simply because they don't like change. It is a knee-jerk reaction that will be displayed by some people no matter what change is announced. These are usually the folks who have longer organizational tenures. If the change is announced in a face-to-face meeting, they are easy to spot because they are leaning back in their chairs and rolling their eyes with their arms crossed.

There are two ways to deal with blind resistance. The first approach is to simply let time pass. As we stated earlier, this kind of resistance is often as much of a reflex as anything else and tends to subside over time. To help accelerate this process, we can engage in the second activity, which is providing as much information as possible about the change. Normally, providing the details to blind resistors will help them realize that it isn't the end of the world. Do not, however, exaggerate, withhold critical information, or lie. These approaches can transform simple blind resistance to the other kinds of resistance, which are much harder to manage.

Political resistance occurs when someone believes they may lose something important to them once the change is implemented. This could be their status, role, power base, or even their job. It doesn't matter if the risk of this loss occurring is real or not. If it seems real enough to them for them to have that fear, it must be dealt with as if it is real and therefore must be managed. This is often one of the most common types of resistance when new IT systems are implemented. This fear is not without precedent. Many system integrators base their business cases on being able to reduce head count in some part of the organization and providing cost reduction in terms of labor costs. There are not too many people with a reasonable tenure in the workforce who have not seen or heard about a scenario like this. Some may even have been on the receiving end of one of these efforts. As such we must be ready to deal with these fears.

So how do we deal with this kind of resistance? Number one is be honest about what might happen. If there is a risk of some people losing their jobs, admit it upfront, and be clear about how those decisions will be made. If the organization has a plan for taking care of the displaced workers, let people know about that. Many organizations like to offer things like buy-out options and such that allow workers who want to leave to be the first ones to do so. Do not promise anything you cannot deliver, and don't look like you are trying to hide things. People can see through that. The more honest, open, and transparent you can be, the better. More often than not, what people imagine might happen is far worse that what is likely to actually happen. The more we can keep those expectations grounded in reality and keep the rumor mill at bay, the better.

The final kind of resistance is ideological resistance. This comes about when someone believes that a particular change is destined to fail, or that implementing a particular change would violate some deeply held values (either the individual's own or the

27

organization's). This kind of resistance is easy to spot because the people displaying this kind of resistance will always follow up their protests with fairly detailed explanations of why they are opposed to the change. As a result, this kind of resistance is usually the most difficult to deal with. Not only do we have to provide details to allay fears, but we have to be ready to logically present these details in persuasive ways that they can understand, often multiple times. The good part about ideological resistance is that most people who engage in this activity care greatly about their organization and are coming from a place of genuinely wanting the best for it. Once their resistance is managed, they normally transform from adversaries to strong advocates.

One of the best examples of this comes from a project that involved the implementation of a customer relationship management (CRM) solution at a Federal government organization. One of the core values of this organization was that it existed not for its own benefit but for that of its constituents. The issue arose because, when setting up CRM systems, some of the key concepts that must be addressed are things like "marketing" and "sales." Many of the senior people in this organization perceived these terms as commercially focused and serving to benefit the organization, not its constituents. As a result, they perceived the whole effort as antithetical to the organization's core values. This resulted in a significant amount of ideological resistance.

How did we manage this resistance? The high-level answer is: very carefully and over time. We created a strategy to help the people in the organization see that the concepts could be applied to this organization without violating the core principles. We also made sure we were very strategic in how we focused our efforts. As we will discuss when we start talking about Awareness and Readiness, we don't have to convince everyone; we just have to convince the right core influencers (Gladwell, 2002). Luckily, the methodology we'll begin discussing in the next chapter helps us do just that.

Journey Management Versus Traditional Change Management

The term "change management" gets thrown around a lot in business. In fact, about the only terms that get thrown around more are "strategy" and "business value." It is all but impossible to pick up a copy of *Harvard Business Review* without finding at least a few articles related to change. Some may be research-based case studies, some may be just relation of personal experience, but their continuous appearance shows just how much of a priority the ability to change is for today's businesses.

While a lot of people are talking about change, not everyone is talking about it in the same way. It is not uncommon for two people within the same organization to understand a change differently based upon their individual contexts. For example, if we use the term "change management" around an operations person, they might think about updates to process documentation or shifts in the reporting boxes that define roles and responsibilities. If we talk about "change management" around an IT person, they're likely to think we mean tracking the modifications of code in some application from one version of the software to the next. If we hear an HR person say "change management," it is very likely that they are referring to the training and communication tasks that are meant to enable the people in that organization to adapt to some kind of change. The funny thing is that all of these definitions may accurately describe an important part of the same change. The trick is not losing sight of any of these perspectives.

This diversity of viewpoints makes change management very useful because it means change management can have a wide variety of applications. Unfortunately, it can also cause confusion and challenges. For starters, as we have already discussed, there can be times when two people may be using the same terms but not meaning the same thing. To make matters worse, they often do not even realize it until a problem arises. An example of this would be when the above-mentioned HR and IT persons try to talk to each other about the change plan. They each agree to develop drafts of the plan and then share them to synchronize and coordinate the details. Since they are approaching the plan from two completely different perspectives, their individual outcomes are focused on completely different details. More often than not, these plans are shared through an e-mail swap rather than a conversation. When each person opens the other's file, they see unfamiliar content and information they may consider less relevant. As a result, they become confused. This confusion can drive frustration. Frustration can limit communication. Without good communication, we end up with scenarios where the various changes, or even individual parts of a large change, occur in a vacuum. This results in uncoordinated activities. Under the best of circumstances a lack of coordination will result in duplicated and wasted efforts. In the worst case, the results can be confusion for employees, conflicting outcomes, and veritable chaos.

One of the key drivers of these issues is that people tend to look at change in terms of a limited set of activities. This inhibits their ability to see the broader impact and understand the overall perspective. The best way to mitigate the risk of these challenges is to evolve how we think about change. Don't just think about change as a set of individual activities. Think about change in terms of the broader journey that the organization is undertaking. In other words, don't just talk about change management approaches that are limited in scope and finite in application, but focus on a holistic *Journey Management* approach that can address the full continuum of outcomes.

This last statement may lead some people reading this to say, "That is neat, but what exactly is journey management?" At the simplest level, *Journey Management is the process of assessing the impacts of major organizational changes across the enterprise, and actively managing those transitions so as to maximize positive results and minimize negative consequences.*

Whenever we share that definition the next question that usually comes up is how *Journey Management* differs from traditional change management. Frankly, there is quite a bit that could be said to answer that question, but we will begin by simply pointing to Figure 1.

Journey Management	Change Management
• Strategic	• Tactical
• Unit of analysis is the whole enterprise	• Unit of analysis tends to be one functional area or project
• Integrates across functional areas and projects	• Tends to have defined boundaries within one functional area or project
• Leads the way	• Tends to be in more of a support role to technology or process changes

Figure 1: Journey Management vs. Change Management

Looking at this table, a couple of things should jump out. The first is that, while change management tends to be tactical and limited in vision, *Journey Management* is strategic and considers the whole enterprise. Let's illustrate this point with the example of an implementation of an SAP Business Suite (formerly known as SAP R/3) solution.

For those not familiar with SAP, it is a very popular brand of ERP software. ERP stands for "enterprise resource planning," and an ERP system is basically a giant computer program used to manage and coordinate the resources, information, and functions of a business. SAP sales reps recommend that their whole system be implemented at once. For better or worse, however, this is rarely the case. More often than not, only one or two modules will be implemented at any given time. For the sake of this discussion, let's assume the portion being implemented is some part of the SAP ERP Financials.

If we were to take a traditional change management approach, we would only focus on the part of the organization where this module will be implemented and the people in that part of the organization who would be using that new software. Our primary change management activities would be training and communication efforts aimed at a limited part of the organization.

The problem with this approach is that there are other people in the organization who will be impacted by the change as well. For example, whenever we change a system, the look and feel of the outputs (e.g., the reports) that the users provide to other people in the organization may be different. This difference can cause confusion that limits the system's usefulness or prevents people from using the system at all. There may be other changes going on in the organization—say, implementation of a CRM system—that could have an impact on or be impacted by this change. Without careful comparison and mapping of these changes, there may be conflicts that can cause critical business disruptions. As we'll learn in subsequent chapters, *Journey Management* actively looks for and manages these challenges.

This looking at the whole organization and managing of these challenges across different functional areas and projects is the basis for the second and third differentiators between *Journey Management* and traditional change management. Going back to the above-mentioned ERP example, let's imagine that the implementation caused a problem where the accounting system was unable to produce the appropriate reports to pay the sales force on time. Since the compensation process would be outside of the direct scope of those using the new accounting system, a classic change management approach would likely miss this impact until it became a problem. A *Journey Management* approach proactively looks for these potential impacts and integrates them into an overall risk management strategy.

This proactivity is based on the fourth differentiator between *Journey Management* and traditional change management. Whereas traditional change management is in a support role for particular projects, *Journey Management* leads the way. Returning again to our ERP example, a traditional change management approach would wait for the accounting issue to come up and then ask the owners of these projects what they would like done. A properly executed *Journey Management* approach identifies that there may be a problem, escalates that problem to the project owners, and recommends actions to be taken. In this case, those actions would probably be a change integration plan with regular meetings to sync things up. Such an approach would limit the negative and maximize the positive impacts of the change on the performance of the organization.

This last point gets to one of the overall assumptions of *Journey Management*. That assumption is that all change should be performance driven. If a change can't be linked to some performance outcome then what is the point of doing it? Finishing up our ERP example, the first reaction of a traditional change management approach is to ask what slides need to be made and what training needs to be delivered. The first reaction of a *Journey Management* approach is to ask what the desired performance outcomes are for that change and then uses those goals to drive the change planning activities.

Does adopting a *Journey Management* approach mean that we abandon time-honored tools and practices from traditional change management? The simple answer is absolutely not. *Journey Management* is not about abandoning what works well from change management. It is about integrating and coordinating all the various change management activities across an enterprise. It is an extension, expansion, and evolution of those activities to drive more successful changes that create observable business results.

This brings up the next important question of how exactly do we manage a "journey"? Our experience shows that there are five major cycles of activities required for successful *Journey Management*. It is important to note that we call them cycles because *Journey Management* is not a one-time linear activity, but an ongoing effort. Each change effort may be at a different cycle and the *Journey Management* approach is to tie all those together. When one change is over, another one is likely to begin. For this reason, we have five cycles rather than five singular activities:

- Awareness: Recognizing the need for change
- Planning: Setting up processes to make it successful
- Readiness: Preparing the organization, the systems, *and* the people
- Coordination: Integrating with other activities
- Execution: Following the plan, measuring the outcomes, and adjusting if necessary

The remainder of this book will look at each cycle in detail.

Cycle 1: Awareness

Using the term "steps" to describe *Journey Management* activities could be a bit misleading as that word suggests a purely linear process where one activity is completed and then we move onto another. In *Journey Management*, one of the key things we recognize is that, while individual changes may have a beginning and an end, there are usually changes that preceded them and there will likely be others that follow. Moreover, in any given organization it is not unusual to find multiple changes occurring simultaneously, and for several of those changes to be at different stages in the lifecycle. Not only that, but within individual changes, certain activities may overlap with the activities that precede or succeed them, or require multiple iterations to meet the needs of the particular organization. As such, the activities for *Journey Management* are referred to as cycles. The first cycle we will discuss is Awareness.

At the most basic level, the Awareness Cycle is about getting the people in the organization to not just *recognize* but also fully *internalize* that there is a need for the change in question. To illustrate the difference between recognition and internalization, think about a person who needs to lose weight. They might *recognize* that they could drop a few pounds when their clothing starts getting tight. They may not, however, fully *internalize* the need to change until they experience some sort of health problems, or get told by their physician that they are at risk. It may even take several reminders for them to accept that a change is really necessary, and to commit to the actions and ongoing effort required to sustain that change. It is not until this *internalization* happens that motivation to make a behavioral change kicks in. Since organizations are made up of people, it should be no surprise that they operate the same way. Of course, motivating one person can be challenging enough. Motivating an entire organization requires much more forethought and planning. The difference between taking these steps and not taking them can dramatically affect the business outcomes.

In an earlier chapter, we discussed the fate of Digital Equipment Corporation (DEC) and how they no longer exist due to the failure of their leadership to internalize that the market was changing and that they needed to change with it (Schein, 2003). Basically, they failed to recognize that an Evolutionary change was impacting their industry. As a result, they refused to make the Strategic or Tactical changes required to adapt. They continued to lose market share until they were no longer viable. The remaining assets were bought by Compaq, which was later bought by Hewlett-Packard. So even though they did not recognize that a change was coming, it still occurred—just not in the way they would have liked, or in a way they could have benefited from if they had been aware and had taken appropriate action.

Delta Airlines on the other hand, became fully aware of its need to make changes. As a result, it began to turn itself around because it not only recognized that it needed to improve how it served its customers, but it also internalized that need such that it changed the day-to-day behavior of its employees (Stych, 2012). While these changes may not have been popular with every single employee, Delta was able to create awareness about the need so that a critical mass of their team internalized the necessity of doing things a new way. This tipped the organization into a new and improved direction (Gladwell, 2002). The question of course, is how does an organization do that?

The first step in creating awareness is determining what is driving the need for the change. Change drivers can be classified into one of two buckets. The first bucket is the external drivers. These external drivers may be evolutionary or punctuated. Evolutionary drivers are movements in the market place that occur over time, such as the shift from land lines to cell phones. Punctuated changes are major disruptions that happen quickly, usually as a result of some critical incident. One of the better examples of this is the implementation of the Sarbanes-Oxley Act as a result of the accounting scandals in the early 21st century. This new law significantly altered the requirements for how publicly-traded organizations track and report their financial outcomes, and forced these companies to implement major change initiatives to stay compliant. Many privately-held companies have begun adhering to these standards as a matter of good business practice. Interestingly, most organizations are more likely to respond to punctuated drivers than evolutionary drivers. This is usually due to the specificity of the required response (e.g., there is a new law in place), but the irony is that the evolutionary external drivers tend to have a broader impact over the long term. As such, they should not be discounted.

Whereas the response to the external drivers could be considered reactive to the market, the response to internal drivers tends to be proactive efforts to achieve some vision or process goal. An example of this would be when a company gets a new CEO who wants to take the organization in a totally new direction because their vision for the company is totally different from that of the last CEO. A process-driven driver might be when there is a shift in some part of the operating model, such as when a company must upgrade its accounting software since the old version is out of date or no longer supported. Obviously, both the internal and external drivers could be mapped to the Tactical, Strategic, and Evolutionary change categories we talked about earlier.

Now that we can classify and define the drivers of the changes, this begs the question of how we go about creating awareness of the changes. The simplest answer is to communicate the needs to the people in the organization. The first response to this statement is usually that organizations have been doing this for years, but the success rate of organizational changes (or lack thereof) suggests that we haven't been doing it right.

The second response to this statement is usually a request to clarify how the *Journey Management* approach differs from traditional change management. We actually had a client once ask, "What are we going to *not* do that we did before?" That, of course, is the wrong question because, just like everything else we've discussed so far with *Journey Management*, we aren't looking to abandon the old approaches that have worked well in the past. What we are talking about doing is expanding and building upon those approaches to be more effective.

We will expand on current practices by changing what we communicate, how we communicate it, and who we communicate with in the Awareness Cycle. In a typical change management approach, senior executives will communicate a "burning platform," describing the risks of staying the same, or they may emphasize their vision of a better future once the change is complete. While this messaging makes perfect sense to the senior leadership, board of directors, and any relevant investors, it doesn't explain to the individuals in the organization why this change is relevant to them, or why embracing it will be to their benefit.

In *Journey Management*, the purpose of initial communication is to provide individuals relevant information that connects the multiple changes to improved organization performance. The goal is to help individuals see the journey, their contribution, and the improved business performance that will result. Instead of communicating executive-level statements that are usually not relevant to an employee's day-to-day work, Awareness begins with targeted communications that are relevant to how an individual's way of working can lead to observable organization performance improvement.

Along with what is communicated, a second difference is how we communicate. *Journey Management* shifts the communication from simply one-way communication to two-way. Instead of sending out memos and e-mails to announce that something is coming, we hold focus groups and conduct surveys to determine if the communication increases understanding and provides information people can use to make choices about how they work. This two-way communication approach not only improves the quality of communication, but it also surfaces important information from employees about their views, their concerns, and the opportunities they see for the organization. By creating awareness through a two-way organizational dialogue, we are able to describe the journey from the employee's viewpoint—not just the executive's viewpoint—and we establish a mechanism for surfacing new information, anticipating roadblocks, and improving communications throughout the journey.

The third way we extend the typical process is to put effort into identifying and actively engaging our key influencers. As we learned from Malcolm Gladwell's *The Tipping Point*, the question is not how much you try to influence, but *who* you try to influence (2002). As such, our focus in the *Journey Management* Awareness Cycle is not so much trying to get all the people in the organization to *internalize* or even fully *recognize* the need for the change, but making sure most people have information about the need for change and that key influencers fully *internalize* that need. Once that is done, the awareness will happen naturally and very, very quickly.

Influencers will *internalize* the need for change if they believe the changes will be rewarding or useful to them and congruent with their value system (Kelman, 1958). A "high-level" vision or burning platform won't typically help influencers internalize the need for change. A personal understanding of how taking different actions (making changes), on the other hand, will lead to improved personal and business performance outcomes. In typical change management there are a handful of senior executives and organization leaders who are "early adopters" because, at the Awareness Cycle, they are the only people with enough information to *internalize* the need for change. In *Journey Management*, we intentionally help influencers at different levels of the organization get the information they need to personally commit to making the needed changes that will result in improved performance outcomes.

Why is it important that the influencers *internalize* the need for change? When an individual *internalizes* the need for change, they will commit actions required to create the expected outcomes, regardless of how peers or authority figures view the changes, even when roadblocks threaten to derail progress. An influencer who has internalized the need for change will demonstrate their commitment in ways others easily observe, which will rapidly expand the awareness of the change and its intended benefits to the broader organization. Our efforts during the Awareness Cycle in *Journey Management* are focused on initiating communications through an organizational dialogue and supporting influencers to *internalize* the need for change and commit to taking actions. Next, we need a plan to ensure the actions being taken will lead us in the direction we intend to go.

Cycle 2: Planning

The great Scottish poet Robert Burns said, "The best-laid schemes o' mice an' men/ Gang aft agley". In other words, even the most well-intentioned efforts can turn out differently than we hope. There are few places where this sentiment is more accurate than with organizational change journeys. This contention is supported by studies that continually show that most organizations do not achieve their change goals. According to *HR Magazine*, only about 30–43% of organizations see their desired results from change efforts (Meinert, 2012). The identified drivers of these shortcomings include budget overruns, schedule slips, lack of user adoption, and "leaders moving onto other projects." While there isn't a whole lot that can be done about senior leaders' attention spans (or lack thereof), issues like budget overruns and scheduling misses can be managed and their negative impacts minimized. The first step towards this goal is proactive, careful planning of the change effort. Planning is the next cycle in our *Journey Management* process.

Before we get too deep into the details of this process, it is important to recognize that most organizations think that they are already planning for their changes. And to a degree they are right. The issue, however, is that most of this planning is focused on transactional or technical aspects, such as code freezes or when data migration will take place. What often gets overlooked are the strategic and human capital aspects of planning the change. The *Journey Management* Planning Cycle addresses this gap through four key activities:

- Defining: Clarifying the vision and goals of the change
- Resourcing: Determining what people, processes, and technology will be required
- Scheduling: Exactly what it sounds like
- Baselining: Defining how you will know if the change is successful, and measuring the current state of performance against those metrics

Defining

The Defining activity is where we come to consensus and *document* the intended outcomes (i.e., the vision) of the change. We also come to consensus and *document* how we will measure the achievement of those intended outcomes (i.e., the goals). By doing this we clarify the strategic intent of a particular change. If we cannot clearly characterize it, then we need to seriously evaluate the value of the effort and whether it is worth the investment.

An important caveat is that the Defining activity is rarely a one-and-done effort. When done properly, it tends to be fairly iterative. It often begins with the involved stakeholders having different viewpoints about the objectives and how to achieve them. In fact, when we look at our experience over the years, we can't think of any examples where at least some part of the stakeholder group had different opinions of the reason for a particular change. As much as this can create challenges, it is important to remember that it is always better to address these issues early—while we still have choices and decisions to make. Waiting until later, after resource and budget decisions have been made, will only create bigger problems.

One way to begin reducing this confusion is through a graphical model that represents the different constructs that come into play in a particular change journey. There is no shortage of these models. There is the Burke-Litwin model, that has something like 13 boxes and 28 connecting lines (Burke, 2002). There is the Integrated Strategic Change (ISC) Model, that is primarily focused on how the change aligns with the organization's strategy (Worley, Hitchin, & Ross, 1996). There is also the Appreciative Inquiry model, that takes a positivistic approach and suggests that if we simply get everyone in the organization excited about the possibilities, the problems will solve themselves (Cooperrider, Sorensen, Yaeger, & Whitney, 2005). Every major consulting firm (e.g., Accenture or McKinsey & Company) has their own, and there are also many, many others.

While the owners of each of these models like to claim that theirs is the end-all, be-all of change models, the truth is that there are so many models of change because each organization is unique and may require a different change strategy. As such, it is extremely rare for any single standardized model to be 100% applicable in all situations. What we find happens more often is that an organization will use a modification of an existing model or create their own from scratch.

While this approach may seem like reinventing the wheel, it has two important benefits. The first benefit is a model that is more tailored to the organization's particular needs, norms, and nomenclature. The other benefit of having a tailored model is that the stakeholders who were involved in refining that model become more invested in it, which in turn makes them more invested in the change effort. Figure 2 and Figure 3 present examples of actual change planning models that we have successfully used in the past.

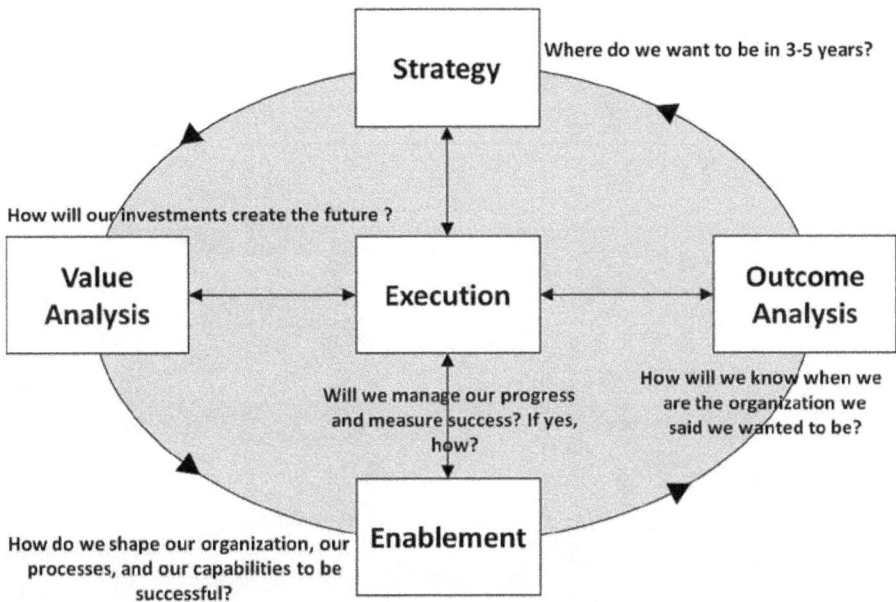

Figure 2: Planning Example #1

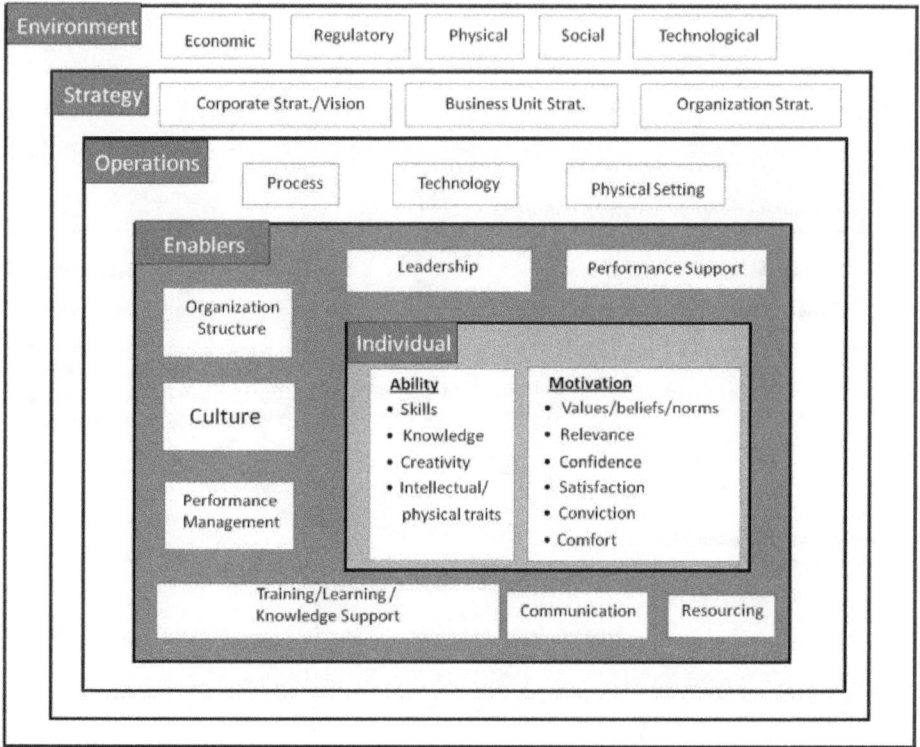

Figure 3: Planning Example #2

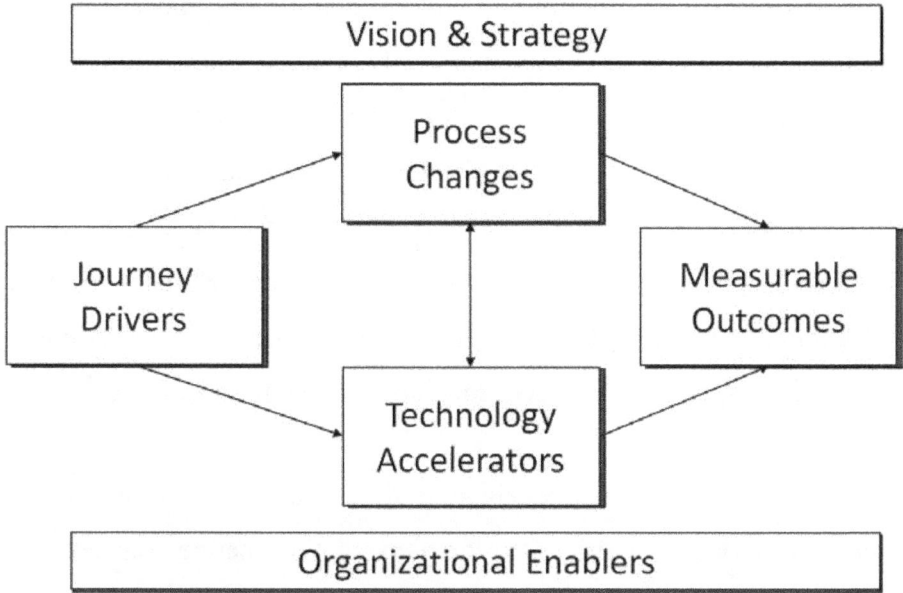

Figure 4: Planning Example #3

All three models come from real consulting engagements, although we have removed any identifying information for confidentiality reasons. In each case, the discussions started with a simple model that looked at the strategy, process, organizational enablers, and technology related to that organization and the change. As you can see, these models quickly evolved to something more aligned with each organization's unique needs. While they are aesthetically different, there are common themes across all the models that should be included in any change model.

The first common theme is that all three models clearly define the *strategic* objective and the organizational *enablers* as distinct units of analysis. This is important because two of the most important questions we can ask at the beginning of a change journey are why we are changing and how we plan to make those changes stick. The answers to these questions should drive our subsequent decisions and efforts. Unfortunately, they are also two of the most overlooked questions, especially in technology-focused changes. By using a model that explicitly includes them, we reduce the risk of this oversight by continually reminding ourselves to keep them in mind.

Another commonality is that they graphically represent the interconnectedness of the different parts of the change journey. Too often these different activities are considered to be independent rather than interdependent. This is especially common in large organizations where the communication between the different parts of the project may be limited. For example, how many times have we seen some large systems integration effort where the system architecture team rarely talked to the deployment team? The answer is far too often. If the different parts of the system are not interacting properly the change effort can't succeed. To keep those different parts interacting properly we need to be mindful of those interrelationships from the start, not after a problem arises.

One technique we often use to further demonstrate the interconnectedness of the different parts of these models is to overlay the different *Journey Management* cycles onto the finalized model. This helps identify any gaps that may need to be addressed. Figure 5 illustrates how this could be approached with Planning Example #3.

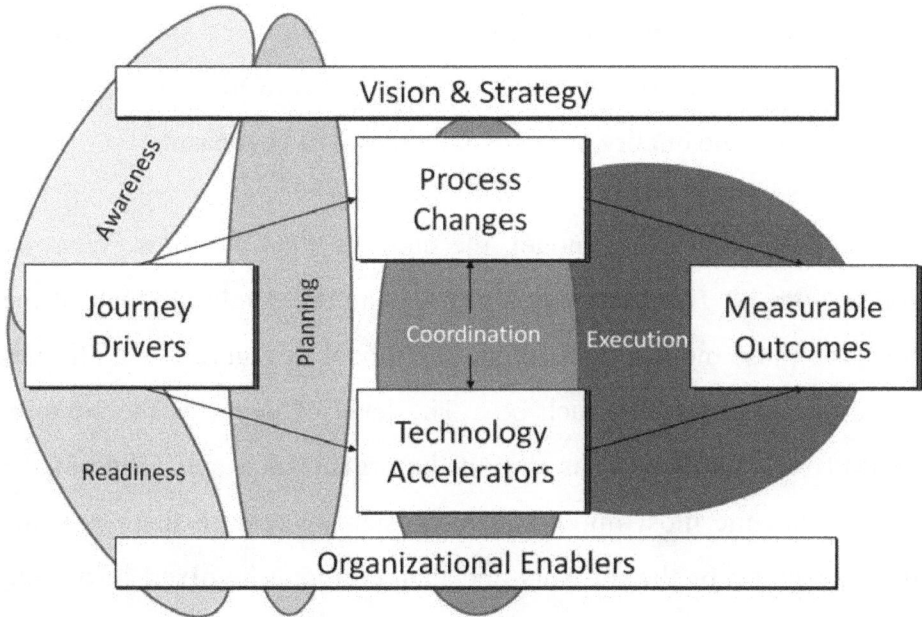

Figure 5: Journey Management Cycles Over Planning Example #3

The third commonality is that they define measureable outcomes as a key part of the effort. While most change efforts do define some sort of outcome objectives, often those outcomes are what we like to call "binary completion measures." This is consultantese for "done or not done." In other words, we check the box and move on. These kinds of objectives include things like "the website is up," or "new commission structure implemented." While completion of a task is a great thing and we can't succeed without it, those kinds of limited measures do not assess the quality or impact of the desired outcomes. Moreover, they do not address the degree to which these outcomes have achieved any kind of meaningful performance goal. Is the website fully functional and user friendly? Did the new commission structure drive the behaviors we wanted in our sales staff? If we're hoping to see these outcomes, the change effort needs to begin with a focus on how the quality of those outcomes will be measured.

Once we have a model, the question then becomes: What do we do with it? The first step is to populate the details of each of the boxes in those models. Notice that the model in Figure 2 actually has those questions next to each box. The level of depth of the answers depends on factors such as size of the organization and scope of the change, but the most important thing is to make sure there is some documentation of the answers and that everyone involved in driving the change at least acknowledges and accepts those definitions (even if they don't enthusiastically agree).

Once we have our model populated, it is time to figure out how to make that vision a reality. To do that, we must determine who will take action, when they will take it, and what the starting points are for those actions. These efforts are referred to as Resourcing, Scheduling and Baselining.

Resourcing

The first step in Resourcing is to develop a task list of what needs to happen within the change effort. The two key inputs for this effort are the finalized model developed in the Defining activity and the operational project plan related to the change effort. While the level of depth and detail of the operational change plan will vary depending on the scope of project and the preference of the person running that effort, there should be one. If there is not, your first task as a journey manager should be to compel the person driving that effort to develop one. If they won't do that, take ownership of the effort and do one for them. We will talk a little more about style and format of these plans when we get to Scheduling, but the important thing to remember is that any project without a plan is very likely to fail. In fact, we have never seen a project succeed without one.

Drawing upon the inputs of our Defining activity and our operational project plan, the next step is to develop a list of tasks that need to occur to make the vision of the change effort a reality. At this point, we don't need these tasks to be down to the day and date level, but just major task-level activities so that we can assign individuals to those actions. This is similar to what is done in most project management approaches, with one key difference: While project management approaches are concerned about assigning resources, the *Journey Management* approach has the additional concern of making sure the *right* person is assigned to that task.

57

Before assigning any person to any particular task, ask three very important questions:

- Does this person have the right skills to do this task?
- Does this person have the bandwidth do to this task?
- Does this person have the right attitude to do this task?

Unless you can honestly answer yes to all three questions, it is probably best to assign someone else. If there is not another option, look at what changes need to be made to this person's skill set or workload so that each "no" becomes a "yes." If it is an attitude issue, consider why it would be in the person's interest to support the effort. By aligning the individual's interests with the change effort, we may effectively influence the person to commit and change their attitude. For example, if the person is an individual contributor, but aspires to be a manager, help them see how managing the resources on this program team will allow them to demonstrate their managerial skills. Someone's attitude can make as much, if not more, difference in how well they contribute to the change than skills or bandwidth can. In fact, we have seen many times that someone with the right attitude can find ways to work around lack of skill or bandwidth, but we've never seen it go the other way around. We have also seen times where someone starts off with a negative attitude towards a change, then begins to see the benefits and becomes one of the efforts biggest advocates.

Scheduling

Once resources have been assigned and are committed, it is time to start scheduling the change activities. At a high level, the schedule for the change activities will mirror the operational change activities. What will be different, however, is that the schedule for the change activities will not only look at what needs to happen, but who needs to know about it, how far ahead they need to know, and any new knowledge or skills that the end users and stakeholders will need to acquire in order to achieve the outcomes and create the business benefit of the change. This information will be critically important when we move to the *Coordination Cycle*.

In an ideal state, this information should be integrated into the operational plan for the change you are trying to manage. There may be times, however, where that is not feasible. For example, we once had a technical solution architect tell us that there was "no reason for all that squishy stuff in a *real* project plan." What did we do? After realizing that it was futile to try to convince this individual to integrate this information into the overall plan, we simply made a shadow plan that mirrored the larger phases of the overall effort but also included the change activities that needed to happen. We even made sure to use the same tool (in this case MS Project) to document the activities. Not surprisingly, the technical side of that project developed some major issues. When it did, we were able to help the solution architect see the value of the change activities and quickly integrate them into the overall effort. As we did, things began going much smoother.

A question we often get at this point is how detailed do these plans need to be. The short answer is: It all depends. Broader and more complex efforts tend to have more detailed plans. Smaller and simpler efforts tend to have less detailed plans. The level of detail should at least mirror the outcome level of the operational plan, although it is not unusual for a change plan to have one or two additional levels of depth. Regardless of the depth of a plan, it should at least include a list of tasks, start and end dates for those tasks, and assigned individuals for those tasks. It is also recommended that whenever possible, the plan should include items such as dependencies and predecessors. This is consistent with the recommendations of the Project Management Body of Knowledge (PMBOK) methodology prescribed by the Project Management Institute (PMI).[1] It is also highly recommend that any operational project plan have a graphical representation that can allow that plan to be easily communicated to those involved and interested (e.g., senior leadership). The most common way to do this is a Gantt chart like what we find in Figure 6.

ID	Task Name	Start	Finish	Qtr 1, 2010	Qtr 2, 2010	Qtr 3, 2010	Qtr 4, 2010
1	BIDW_implementation_project_plan2	1/18	11/24				
2	Definition phase	1/18	1/27				
3	Conduct preliminary investigation and start-up	1/18	1/27				
15	Requirements phase	1/25	3/19				
16	Capture data requirements	1/25	3/12				
33	Capture technical requirements	2/9	3/3				
39	Document Business, Data and technical Requiremen	3/4	3/9	DD[50%]			
40	Document history load requirements	3/12	3/12	DD			
41	Update Technical Architecture Doc	3/15	3/18	DD,JVDW			
42	Approve and sign-off business, data and technical re	3/19	3/19	JB[50%],DSI[50%]			
43							
44	Architecture phase	3/29	5/12				
45	Define/evolve data architecture	3/29	4/13				
56	Define/evolve data integration (DI) architecture	4/14	5/12				
75	Define/evolve information delivery architecture	4/13	4/26				
86	Define/evolve technical architecture	4/27	5/3				
94	Define/evolve metadata architecture	4/27	5/6				
104	Business User Briefing Session	5/13	5/13		JB[50%]		
105	Analysis phase	2/8	4/23				
703	Design phase	3/1	8/10				
804	Construction phase	4/13	8/31				
837	Testing phase	5/18	9/10				
838	Execute system test cycle	5/18	8/26				
853	Execute UAT test cycle	8/27	9/10				
865	Deployment phase - Go Live	3/19	9/15				
866	Train and deploy	9/13	9/15				
867	Establish or update production environment	9/13	9/13				SC[50%],DSI[50%
868	Migrate database, information delivery, and DI c	9/13	9/13				SC[25%],DSI[25
869	Conduct end-user training and capture feedback	9/14	9/14				SC[25%],DSI[25
870	Perform initial run(s)	9/15	9/15				ET1[25%],DSI[2!
871	Perform regular cycle run(s)	9/15	9/15				ET2[25%],DSI[2!
872	Certify data and metadata	9/15	9/15				JB[25%],DSI[25
873	Turnover system to operations and support	9/15	9/15				SC[25%],DSI[25
874	Obtain sponsor sign-off	9/15	9/15				9/15
875	Business and Technical Requirements Complete	3/19	3/19	3/19			
876	History Load (post Go Live)	9/30	11/24				D!
877							
878	Retire the temporary Oracle Server	3/1	4/12				

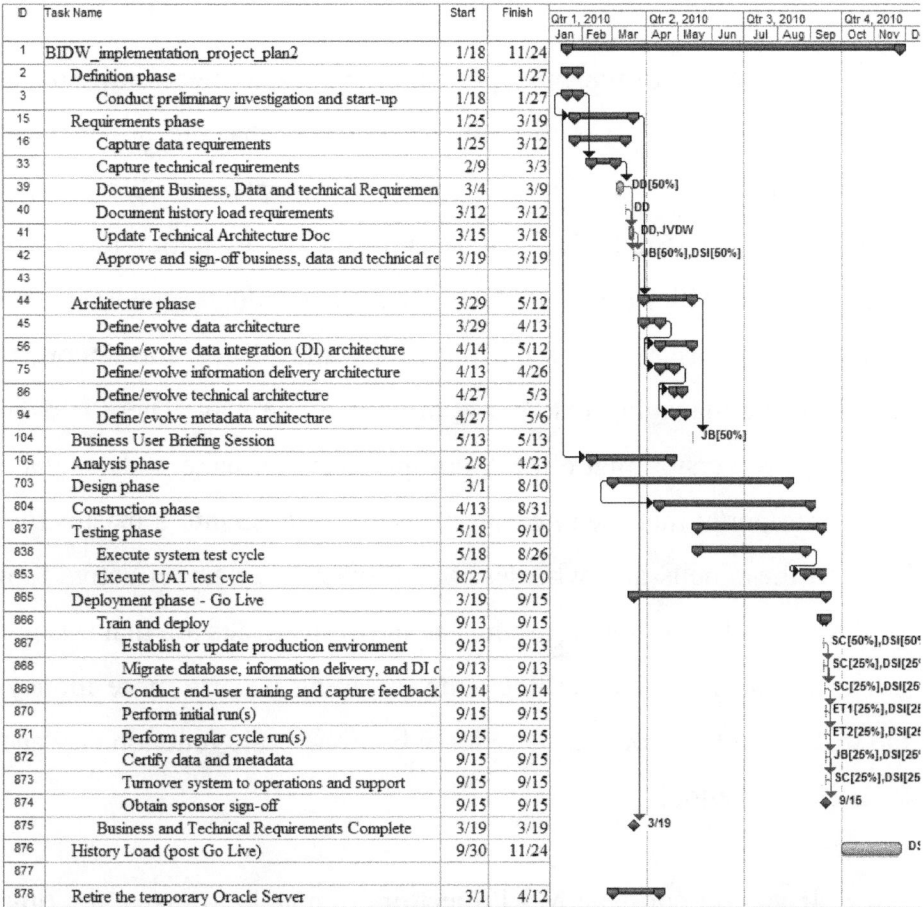

Figure 6: MS Project Gantt Chart Example

While the text of Figure 6 may be a bit small to read, those details are not a concern here as this image is simply meant to be an illustration of the basic output of a MS Project file. Many of these files have hundreds if not thousands of task lines and often need to be printed out on 14 x 11 inch paper to even begin to be readable. There are numerous features in MS project files, but many users do not go beyond the Gantt chart view.

Having lots of lines in a project plan does not necessarily mean it has a lot of depth. It is the number of levels that the project plan drills down that influences how deep our change plans should go. It is highly recommended to have at least this level of depth for every change effort. MS Project is very robust and allows you to create dependencies, has a ton of built-in tools, and allows for important activities like managing resourcing in a proactive way. There is even an enterprise version that allows multiple users to make updates via a web-based portal that then synchronizes all of those into a master file. With all these bells and whistles, MS Project is a very effective tool for those who know how to use it. The only drawbacks are that it is not part of the standard MS Office suite, meaning it costs more money, and that it can take some time to learn both the basic functionality and the tricks of the tool.

If you do not have MS Project or are unable to invest the time into learning to use it, MS Excel can also be used. It lacks many of the advanced features of MS Project but still gets the job done. There are even a number of free templates that you can download from various websites, or just play around with for a while.[2] Figure 7 shows an example of a project plan in MS Excel.

Activity	Per. Comp	Resource	EST St.	EST End	Act. St.	Act. End	8/13	8/20	8/27	9/3	9/10	9/17	9/24	10/1
							Work Weeks (All dates are Mondays)							
METERICS ALIGNMENT OVERALL PROJECT CHANGE PLAN*	53%						*			*			*	
Kick Off	100%	Bob, Sue & Joe	8/16	8/16	8/16	8/16	■							
Baseline Current State	66%													
CHC Level Baseline	100%													
Document CHC Strategic Objectives	100%	Bob	8/13	8/24	8/13									
Document CHC Strategic Initiatives	100%	Bob	8/13	8/24	8/13									
Document CHC KPIs	100%	Bob	8/13	8/24	8/13									
Document CHC Skill Sets	100%	Bob	8/13	8/24	8/13									
Identify CHC Key Influencers	100%	Bob	8/13	8/24	8/13									
C4L Level Baseline	54%													
Document C4L Strategic Initiataives	75%	Bob	8/13	8/31	8/13									
Document C4L Programs	75%	Bob	8/13	8/31	8/13									
Document C4L Measures	75%	Bob	8/13	8/31	8/13									
Identify Activities not tied to C4L Strategic Initiatives	50%	Bob & Sue	8/16	8/31	8/16									
Identify measures for activates not tied to C4L Initiatives	50%	Bob & Sue	8/16	8/31	8/16									
Align activities and measures to C4L Programs and Strategic Objectives	25%	Bob, Sue & Joe	8/27	9/14										
Deep dive review all measures assess alignment to C4L & CHC initiatives and categorize measures (e.g., quantitative, qualitative, leading or lagging)	25%	Bob, Sue & Joe	8/27	9/14										
Document C4L Skill levels	25%	Bob, Sue & Joe	8/27	9/14										
Identify C4L Key Influencers	25%	Bob, Sue & Joe	8/27	9/14										
Document Current State Including Gaps, Overlaps and Outliers	50%	Bob & Joe	9/10	9/22										
*Document Existing Measurement Processes***	25%													
Identify Processes to document	75%	Bob	9/3	9/28										
Catalog existing Tools and Templates	50%	Bob & Team	9/3	9/28										
Complete Process Documentation (work estimate may change depending on number of processes)		Bob & Team	9/10	10/5										
Complete SIPOCs for Existing Processe	25%	Bob & Team	9/10	10/5										
Review Avaialble Tools and Templates	25%	Bob & Team	9/10	10/5										
Improve Existing Processes		Bob & Team	10/1	11/2										
Identify opportunities to improve Existing Process	0%	Bob & Team	10/1	11/2										
Update proces Info	0%	Bob & Team	10/1	11/2										
Finalize Existing Process Documentation	0%	Bob & Joe	10/29	11/9										

Figure 7: MS Excel Project Plan Example

While these are the two main formats for these kinds of plans, there are others. We have seen people just use big arrow on Power Point, and even once saw someone take a huge piece of butcher paper on the office wall with colored strips of paper that could be moved around with thumb tacks. We actually don't recommend that last one as it doesn't allow for a lot of functionality or collaboration. It can't be e-mailed, it can't be printed out, and it can't be baselined. It is, however, a significant improvement over nothing.

Baselining

It is not a secret that change plans grow, change, and evolve over time. This is a natural part of the process. There will be shifts in priorities and resources. There will be unanticipated roadblocks. Simply put, corporate life will get in the way. Sometimes these shifts are small and inconsequential, and other times they will be major concerns. When they are major concerns, it is important to be able to compare the evolved plan to the original plan and make sure that we are still on target to reach our stated objectives—or, if we are not on target, to be able to communicate that to the appropriate stakeholders, along with how we got there and what we might be able to do to get back on track. Baselining is a key data point in these discussions.

In the simplest of terms, baselining is just taking a snapshot of the final original change plan and keeping it available to compare to evolved plans at a later date. It is no more or no less than that. Because of this simplicity, is it also fairly easy to forget to do. We once heard a client's project manager (PM) compare baselining to flossing. When we ask for further explanation, the expanded description was that it was not hard to do and often forgotten, and people don't realize how important it is until something bad has happened. At that point they really wish they could go back in time and do it. Ironically, this particular PM made this statement during an initial meeting with us where we had been brought in to help fix a project that had gone off course in multiple ways. One of our first requests was to see the baselined change plan. That request is what led to this colorful insight.

So how does one baseline? PMBOK has a host of information on this related to cost baselines, technical baselines, and many other similar techniques. This information is useful for managing a huge multi-year project across multiple countries or studying for the Project Management Professional (PMP) exam, but it is frankly overbuilt for what we are doing here. Our recommended approach offers two much simpler techniques. The decision point of which one to use is really a function of whether one is using MS Project or MS Excel.

If using MS Project, the recommended approach is simply to use the built-in baselining function.[3] It is actually quite robust and very useful when used properly. How does this work? It is basically a built-in functionality that keeps a running record stored within your MS Project file. It is kind of like the backup function in Quickbooks or any other accounting software. What steps are required to do this? That answer is a little more complicated and can vary a bit depending on which particular version of MS Project you are using. Luckily, if you go to Google and type in the words "MS Project Baseline" about 1.8 million results will come up. Usually the first one is from the Microsoft website, and the next few are YouTube videos that take you through step by step. That should be more than enough to get you started. The one bit of advice we will offer is do a couple of test baselines before doing it for real as it will take a couple of tries to get this right.

Saving a baseline in MS Excel is even simpler. Go to *File -> Save As* and then just change to a new file name that ends in "baseline" and the date or something like that. If you are worried you might accidentally change it later, there are two options to help make it more permanent. The first is to make it a Read-Only file. The easiest way to do this is to go to the Office Button in the upper left corner of the screen, got down to *Prepare*, and then select *Mark as Final*. Another way to do this is simply to save the baseline as a PDF. This way it cannot be edited. These approaches will not provide you with all the fancy comparative capabilities that we would have using MS Project, but placing printed versions of the baseline and the current project plan side by side on a desk should allow you to compare them well enough to at least know where the project is. If it sounds simple, that is the intent.

So now that we've defined our goals, identified our resources, documented our schedule and established our baseline; the question becomes: What do we do next? The simple answer is that it is time to begin getting the organization *ready* for the change. Readiness is the focus of our next chapter.

Brown & Royston

Cycle 3: Readiness

We expend a lot of energy worrying about ourselves and others being ready. As children, we are asked by our parents if we're ready for dinner, and afterwards tell us to get ready for bed. In school, we ask our classmates if they are ready for the big test. If we're in a relationship, we ask our partners if they're ready to go yet. And for some reason a man named Michael Buffer is constantly telling people "Let's get ready to rumble!" Clearly, being "ready" is a very important part of our lives.

Given how much importance we place on being ready, it is fascinating that readiness is all but ignored in organizational change efforts. More often than not, it doesn't get much thought. Too often, the thought we do give it is little more than lip service. While there are a multitude of opinions as to why this is the case, this lack of attention is often a function of what we like to call the "Field of Dreams Fallacy." For those not familiar with this 1989 "classic" film, a corn farmer starts hearing voices telling him, "If you build it, they will come," which causes him to build a baseball diamond in his field. After he builds the field, a bunch of baseball-playing ghosts appear and somehow a happy ending results.

Far too many organizational change efforts try to follow a similar formula. They operate under the delusion that if we just switch over the software or tell people to start using a new process the people will adapt to, adopt, and embrace that change. In other words, we have somehow convinced ourselves that "if you build it, they will come."

Unfortunately, this approach does not work. The reason it doesn't work is that employees and leaders see current practices as the "path to success," or at least the path that they are most comfortable with. They don't realize that what works today won't lead to success tomorrow, or that there is some major benefit to making the change. As a result, it is not enough to build it and wait for them to come. This position is supported by both practical experience and empirical research.

Given all this, it is easy to conclude that the Field of Dreams Fallacy is a real phenomenon that can damage an organization and needs to be managed. As such, let's put a stake in the ground that readiness is something that must be actively addressed and cultivated. If we accept this premise, then we have to start asking the questions of what readiness is, and how we promote it. Once we know those answers, we can begin taking steps to increase the readiness of people in our organizations and significantly increase the likelihood that our change effort will lead to the expected business outcomes.

Defining what readiness really means is situational because the circumstances of the change, as well as the perceptions of the employees, can vary drastically from organization to organization, and from change to change. In one case, readiness may be largely a matter of training people to be able to properly use an SAP application. In other cases, readiness may simply be a matter of teaching people in the organization to understand how some new law that impacts their work (e.g., Sarbanes-Oxley or the Affordable Care Act). While the details can be fairly disparate, there are certain common indicators of readiness that we look for across all changes:

- The organization is prepared to take the actions needed to stop or alter existing practices, adopt new practices, and cause the expected business benefit of the change.
- The people in the organization are equipped to take the actions they need to take as part of the change.
- There is a critical mass of key individuals who are willing to take actions required to cause the change and expected business benefit and are also committed to influencing others to take required actions.

Preparing an organization for the changes is closely related to the activities of the Planning Cycle, but the difference here is that we take a broader view of the change effort and think about how it impacts and/or will be impacted by the whole organization. As with most activities, in change management there are a number of different ways to address this. But in our *Journey Management* model, we begin with the readiness assessment that asks specific questions across the six key domains. Figure 8 illustrates examples of the kinds of questions we would ask for a systems-focused change.

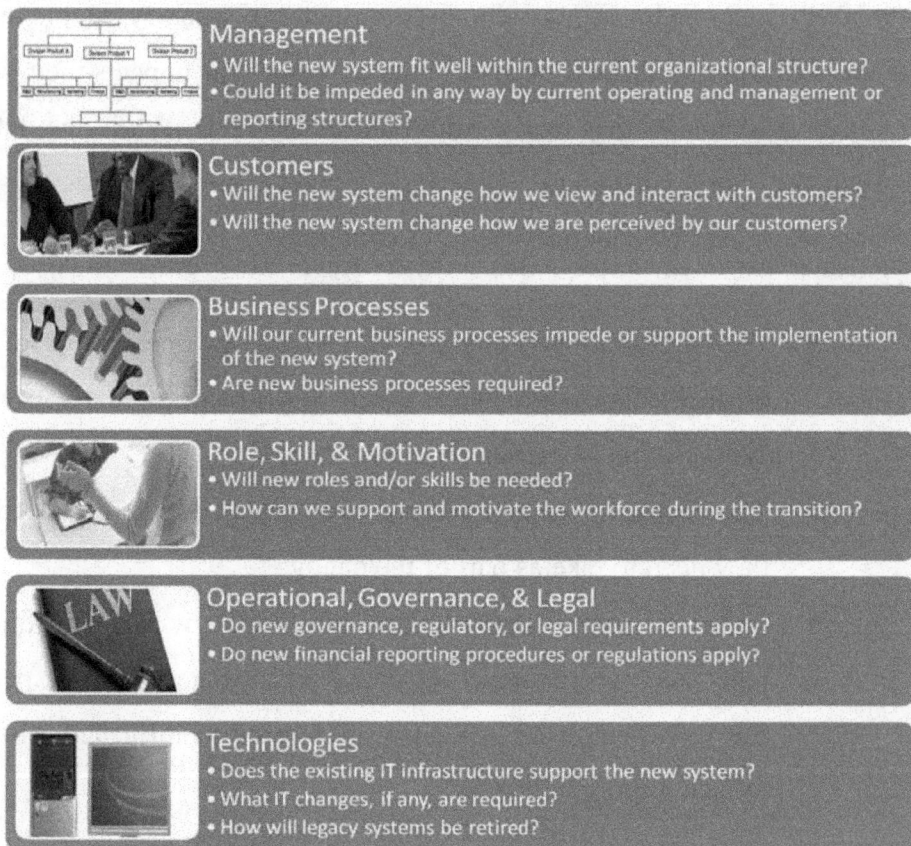

Management
• Will the new system fit well within the current organizational structure?
• Could it be impeded in any way by current operating and management or reporting structures?

Customers
• Will the new system change how we view and interact with customers?
• Will the new system change how we are perceived by our customers?

Business Processes
• Will our current business processes impede or support the implementation of the new system?
• Are new business processes required?

Role, Skill, & Motivation
• Will new roles and/or skills be needed?
• How can we support and motivate the workforce during the transition?

Operational, Governance, & Legal
• Do new governance, regulatory, or legal requirements apply?
• Do new financial reporting procedures or regulations apply?

Technologies
• Does the existing IT infrastructure support the new system?
• What IT changes, if any, are required?
• How will legacy systems be retired?

Figure 8: Readiness Assessment Categories

So what do we do with this model in terms of making an organization more ready for a change? Our first step is usually to hold a facilitated session with the key stakeholders and review each of the questions in Figure 8. The goal of this session is to come to consensus around answers to each of these questions. Some answers may require a large amount of detail. Others may simply note that this particular change does not impact, or is not impacted by, that particular aspect of readiness. These answers are then documents in what we usually call the "Readiness Requirements Document." The particular style and format of the Readiness Requirements Document is usually tailored to the particular organization, and in a few cases we may even change the title, such as when working with the Department of Defense where "readiness" has other very specific connotations related to troop preparedness. Regardless of the look and feel of the document, the consistent goal continues to be capturing the specific outcomes and impacts of the anticipated change.

Once we have our readiness requirements documented, the next step is determining the degree to which the people in the organization are equipped to deal with those requirements. Assessing and preparing people for Readiness is similar to the assessment we conducted during the Resourcing phase of the Planning Cycle. The difference, however, is that our focus is not just on people implementing the change, but on anyone who will be impacted by the change. We make this assessment by gathering information from people in the organization. In smaller organizations, we may conduct facilitated focus groups. In larger organizations, surveys are usually much more efficient. Regardless of the data collection method, our intent is to identify and document any deltas between where the people in the organization are and where they need to be. Based upon these insights we can then develop readiness strategies to close those gaps.

It should not be surprising that data from these efforts usually indicates that the people in most organizations tend to be less ready than the stakeholders anticipate. This is one of the few truly consistent things about organizational changes. Another consistency is that the stakeholders' reactions show some degree of surprise at the results. Depending upon the culture of the organization and the size of the gaps, those reactions can vacillate anywhere from begrudging acceptance to outright protesting disbelief. And about a third of the time, the reactions will be the exact opposite of what you expect. As such, our recommendation is to always let the data drive these conversations and let the stakeholders process however they need to.

Regardless of the nature of these reactions, our next step is to use the information gathered to decide where to focus our Readiness efforts by answering additional questions:

- Where is the change most likely to fail? Why?
  - o Is it significantly different than today's ways of working?
  - o Is the technology unlikely to deliver expected outcomes?
  - o Is there some perception that the expected change will contradict our mission or values?

- What will it look like if people are "ready"?
- What actions do we believe will cause people to be "ready"?
  - Training
  - Conducting two-way dialogues
  - Connecting change to individual interests/goals
  - Presenting a clear picture of steps along the way and expected business benefits caused by the changes
  - Waiting: i.e., they simply decide to engage

As we cultivate readiness and manage other aspects of the journey, remember that "change" is caused by someone deciding to do something different to create a different outcome. In the case of *Journey Management*, it is many people deciding to take several different actions, to create multiple outcomes for a business. As much as we would like to, we cannot "make" people ready or "make" them change, you can only help people see different choices and influence them to choose to take action.

When we have clarified what readiness looks like across the organization and decided which actions we believe will cultivate readiness, we must address the degree to which the affected people are willing to accept the change and choose to do something differently. There is an interesting dynamic with this step in that many organizations either completely overlook it, or think that they have to get *every single person* onboard with the change. The truth, however, is that neither of these will get you to the needed outcome.

When cultivating readiness for a change, it is not just a matter of giving people the skills and knowledge of what needs to be done. We also have to help them connect the benefits of the change to their interests so that they will choose to take the action. It is like the old saying about leading a horse to water. When dealing with a group of people in an organization, we don't have to lead every horse to water, we just have to lead the right horses to water and provide them compelling reasons to drink. If the influencers recognize the benefits, take actions, and it works for them, others will follow suit.

If we go back to Gladwell's *The Tipping Point* (2002), one of the key differentiators to any successful change is gaining buy-in from key influencers. These key influencers are the people who choose to take different actions and experience different outcomes early in the journey. The undecided or uninterested will take notice of the key influencers' experiences and begin to accept that doing what needs to be done can lead to good outcomes. Sure, there will always be a small minority who don't notice or care about creating the change, but we frankly do not focus effort on them because it is unlikely we can gain their buy-in anyway. And there is a pretty good chance they will leave the organization before long because they don't have the skills, capability, or attitude to succeed in the changed organization. So why waste the effort? Effective *Journey Management*, will help you avoid wasted effort in many ways, as we will learn when we start talking about the Coordinating Cycle.

Cycle 4: Coordinating

There are a multitude of metaphors for managing change. Some people say it is like rowing upstream. Others compare it to controlled chaos. A client of ours once described it as conducting an orchestra, but with everyone's sheet music out of order. One of the better examples comes from the early 2000s when EDS (now part of Hewlett-Packard) made a television commercial about herding cats, which can now be found online.[4] The basic idea was that we often have a lot different elements going in a lot of different directions, much of which can't be fully controlled.

As silly as this commercial seems, it should strike a chord with anyone who has ever had to manage a large change. Conflicting schedules, competing priorities, and semi-hidden agendas can all make driving an organization towards its desired outcomes seem pretty close to corralling feral felines. Throw in competition for scarce budget and overworked people who have to complete change tasks in addition to their day jobs, and it becomes very easy to see why so many change efforts fall down.

So how do we address these challenges? As we have already discussed, one of the key assumptions of *Journey Management* is that we have to approach these efforts not as independent activities but as an integrated, coordinated program. We have to force ourselves to account for the forest and not just the trees (please excuse the overused analogy), and more importantly help others in our organizations do the same thing. This is the focus of our Coordinating Cycle, and one of the most important differentiators between *Journey Management* and traditional change management.

Traditional change management tends to look at each change as a self-contained unit. *Journey Management* expands upon that focus to look at the integration of multiple change activities across the organizational entity and, when possible, its full ecosystem. This enhanced perspective is critical for the success of an organization because the conflict of multiple changes is often one of the key drivers in the failure of these efforts. The number and scope of changes may increase as the organization grows and becomes more complex, but even the smallest organization may have multiple shifts impacting it at once. Moreover, research has continually shown that the ability to manage the integration of these changes is a key determinant of organizational success (Worley, Hitchin, & Ross, 1996).

Typically, the possibility of these changes negatively impacting each other is not even considered until we have multiple changes going live at once. Unfortunately, this is when things tend to go the most wrong. For example, let's assume that an organization is putting a new accounting system online while a new, unrelated accounting rule goes into effect. The people in the new accounting department not only have to learn to use a new system, but must become familiar with a whole new set of rules that impacts how they do their jobs. As any accounting person can attest, either change by itself could cause disruption. The two changes together are orders of magnitude more complicated. As we once heard a client exclaim, "This isn't double trouble; it's more like trouble squared."

The problems that result from multiple changes impacting at once do not occur only when two or more changes are being managed within a single department. In fact, it should not be surprising that it is more complicated when things are occurring across two different departments. It is also more common. For example, let's imagine that an organization is implementing a travel management system. At same time there, is a totally unrelated effort to implement a new customer relationship management (CRM) system. Both systems are scheduled to go live within a week of each other. There is little interaction between the two systems because they are managed out of separate cost centers, they are on completely different platforms, and the functionalities appear to be totally unrelated. As such, there appears to be no need to consider any coordination between the two—that is, unless you are a salesperson who has to use both the travel management and the CRM systems on a daily basis. Suddenly you are hit with two completely new systems that you have to figure out at the same time, while still taking care of your clients and generating new business. So what do you do? If you're like most people, you figure out a workaround that often involves using the old systems as long as you can. This can usually go on for several months until someone else realizes that people aren't adopting the new system. This then gets reported to the executive sponsor of the new system who decides that the old system will be turned off at some arbitrary date, and then critical data becomes lost. And that is when things get really "fun."

So what do we do to help avoid scenarios like these? There have been a lot of different attempts to answer that question over the years. Some have worked out better than others. One approach that we have found to be very effective is the application of a Change Integration Map (CIM). The CIM is pretty much what it sounds like. It is a graphic representing the changes landscape so that people can quickly see the interactions.

When we mention a CIM people usually try to imagine what one would look like. They often describe visions of some kind of huge spider web of lines and numbers and dates that causes confusion and eye sores. That image is not surprising because, the first few times we tried to put one together, that is basically what came out. Looking at some of those old attempts, it is easy to see why many people all but give up on managing change at the programmatic level. After some trial and error, however, we came up with a more workable model something that looks like what we see in Figure 9.

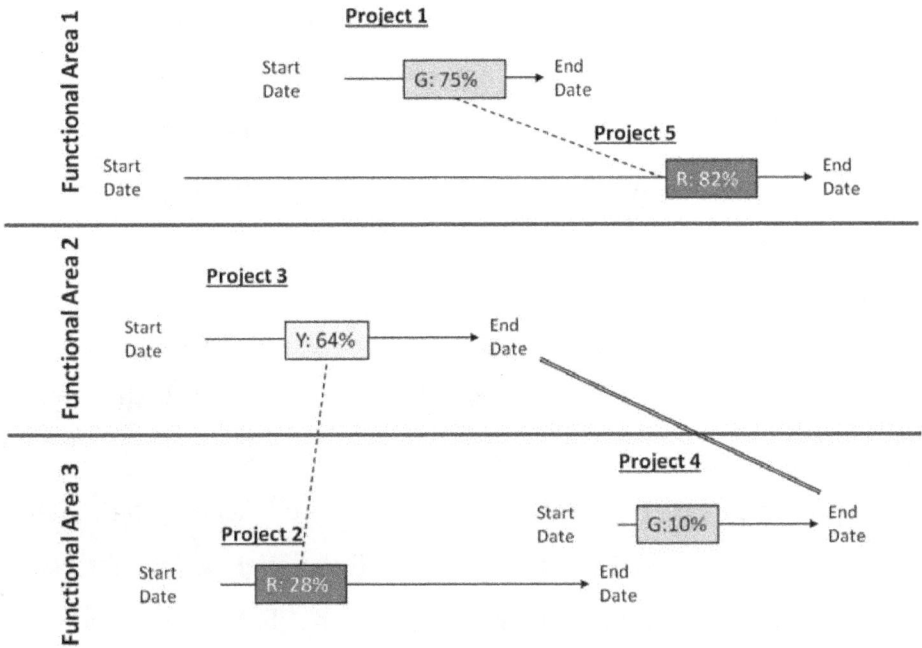

Figure 9: Change Integration Map Example

We will get into more detail about the contents of the CIM and how to read one shortly, but before we do that, it would help to provide some context on how these are used. It is not unusual to see these CIMs printed out on plotter paper and tacked up on the walls around a given office. When most people first see one, they ask what it is. Once it is explained they usually comment something like, "Hey, that's kind of simple," then ask if it has all the necessary information. The short answer is yes it does; the simplicity is intentional, as the convoluted attempts never seem to add as much value as the effort it takes to put them together. Moreover, when you have to re-explain it every time there is an update, that kind of defeats the purpose. While there is a lot of supplemental information that could be added, our experience shows that this approach includes the most critical information for these kinds of activities. The significance of this critical information usually becomes apparent as we explain how to read the CIM.

Starting from the left, we see the "Functional Areas." The functional area is just a generic term for a department or division or something like that. If this were a real CIM, the term "Functional Area" would be replaced with terms like Accounting, Sales, Marketing, and/or HR. The specific functional areas for each organization can vary. Larger organizations have more. Smaller organizations tend have fewer. The key is that they should reflect how the organization manages itself. Often we select these around executive level cost centers, but it really depends on the particular organization. Obviously, most organizations have more than three functional areas, but Figure 9 is for illustration purposes so we won't worry about that here.

Within each functional area, the change projects (e.g., process, people, and/or technology) within that area are identified. If there is not a change project for a particular functional area, it would be blank. As we've already discussed, however, that would be rare for any organization of a reasonable size. Each project has a "Project Name" (e.g., SAP R3 Implementation), as well as a "Start Date" (e.g., January 15, 2013) and "End Date" (e.g., June 9, 2013). To avoid confusion, each project name should be unique.

We were once in a kick-off meeting where someone asked what to do if two projects had the same name. The very simple answer was to change one of the names. Having two projects with the same name can cause confusion, and the goal of all this is to reduce confusion. Determining which project has to change their name and which one gets to keep their name can be tricky, and can often comes down to an issue of organizational politics. Our recommendation is to try to avoid getting side-tracked by those. The best way to do that is to focus everyone on what the project is delivering and why it was undertaken.

The start and end dates of each project should be roughly aligned so that projects that start/end on the same date line up vertically, they don't need to be exactly exact. They just need to be to where people can understand the overall relationships. Earlier dates that are closer to now go on the left. Later dates are further to the right. The CIMs should be updated at least monthly so that they remain relatively current, although we have seen then done as often as weekly.

The real value of the CIM comes from the colored boxes and the lines that show the connections between the different projects. For each project, there is a colored box with a percentage in it. That number is the overall percentage complete of the project. There are several different ways to calculate percentage complete and we have seen different organizations use just about all of them at one time or another. We do not recommend any particular method for calculating percentage complete as long as the approach is mostly consistent within the organization.

The color of the boxes is simply the status of the project as green (G), yellow (Y), or red (R). These should line up to the basic "stop light" status reporting that many organizations use to provide executive updates. If the organization does not have status reporting for each project, start using it. Figure 10 provides a simple example of a project status report for reference.

Project	Status	Details
<u>Project Name</u> Sponsor: Name Manager: Name Change Lead: Name Start date – End Date % Complete One paragraph description of project	G	<u>Updates</u> · Point 1 · Point 2 · Point 3 <u>Milestones</u> · Point 1 · Point 2 · Point 3 <u>Integration, Coordination, & Conflict Points</u> · Point 1 · Point 2 · Point 3 <u>Dependencies</u> · Point 1 · Point 2 · Point 3 <u>Issues & Risks</u> · Point 1 · Point 2 · Point 3

(G) Limited Issues   (Y) Minor Issues   (R) Major Issues

Figure 10: Sample Project Status Report

The criteria for what constitutes a red, yellow, or green may vary from organization to organization, but as long as they are internally consistent and everyone has a consistent idea of what those colors mean, it doesn't really matter. What does matter is being able to quickly see the status of each project. For example, in the case of Project 5 in Figure 9, we know that it is pretty close to done (85%), but we can also see that it is red, meaning that it has some major problems.

Project 1, by comparison, is also pretty close to done (75%) but is green, so we can be confident that it is moving along well. There may be some internal political issues that come about with each project's status being shared so publically, but as time goes on, people realize that sharing this information helps them meet milestones, avoid surprises, and achieve goals. After this realization, people become comfortable with the process.

The lines between projects indicate relationships and dependencies. Typically, no line means no relationship. A dotted line means a weak relationship. For example, in Figure 9, the outcomes of Project 3 may have some impact on Project 2, but not having Project 3 done will not prevent the completion of Project 2. A solid line means a strong relationship or a dependency. A double solid line means a very strong dependency. Going back to Figure 9, we can assume that Project 4 cannot finish until Project 3 is done because there is a double solid line between the two. Of course with Project 3 being yellow, we'll need to do some strong execution to make sure there are not major issues impacting two projects. Managing that execution will be the focus of our last cycle, which will be covered in the next chapter.

Cycle 5: Executing

Now that everyone is aware that the change is coming and we have done our planning, done what we can to ready the organization, and set up our coordination process, it is time to start Executing. In simplest terms, the Executing Cycle is about applying the resources to achieve some specific outcomes. More importantly, it is about trying tie those outcomes to specific business objectives that are intended to drive better performance related to the change effort. This outcome focused approach is another key differentiator of a *Journey Management* approach. We are not trying to execute outcomes for the sake of themselves. We are making sure that each outcome is clearly defined and performance driven: *If it doesn't improve performance, why do it?* More importantly, we are making sure that everyone involved is aware of and driving towards those objectives as well.

A lot of what we will cover here may sound familiar to those have experience with the Project Management Institute's PMBOK and other project management methodologies. That is not surprising given that these activities are related and should occur in concert. In fact, the casual observer may have a hard time differentiating between this and the PMBOK methodology. Taking a deeper look at both approaches, however, will reveal that there are subtle but important differences. For example, while PMBOK has a wide variety of tasks and is primarily focused on the transactional nature of project execution, the *Journey Management* approach is focused on the strategic aspects of the effort and three tasks:

- Managing the risks and issues
- Driving towards defined performance outcomes
- Measuring the impact of the outputs on the outcomes of the project and the organization

Does this mean that the transactional tasks we find in methodologies such as PMBOK are not important? Absolutely not. In fact, the *Journey Management* approach considers them very important. Just like what we discussed in the Planning Cycle earlier, this discussion is based on the assumption that there will be tactical program and project managers who will be focused on those activities. The organization may even have a program management office (PMO) set up to oversee these activities. If these capabilities are not resident within your organization, it is highly recommended that the journey manager become the champion for instituting those capabilities. We have even seen scenarios where organizations set up *Journey Management Offices* (JMOs) that are focused on the strategic and organizational change activities, while allowing the individual projects to focus on the tactical transitions. For now, however, we will assume they exist and proceed with the remainder of this discussion under that assumption.

Managing Risks & Issues

At the most basic level, managing risks and issues is about taking steps to identify bad things that could happen, creating mitigation strategies to reduce the likelihood that they will happen, and having a management plan for when they do happen. No more, no less.

It would be difficult to estimate the exact percentage of project failures that have been primarily the result of poor risk management since most studies that look at project failures classify those drivers in terms of things like lack of communication, poorly defined requirements, and lack of leadership support. It does not take a huge leap of logic, however, to conclude that had those issues been identified through a proper risk management process and managed, they could have been addressed or at least their impact reduced. Anyone who has had any exposure to project management and change management can think of at least a few examples of where this would be the case. As such, it is easy to see why risk and issue management is so important.

Whenever we deliver a *Journey Management* training session, we usually begin our risk and issue section by asking everyone in the class to sit back and think for five minutes about examples of where they have seen this go poorly. No one is allowed to talk to other people, just sit and think. More often than not, people will begin by staring off into space without much reaction. After about a minute or two, most people begin to really consider this idea. It is easy to tell when that happens because their brows begin to furrow, and there are usually a few sighs and head shakes. Suddenly everyone becomes very serious about trying to get a handle on these activities. If you're not sufficiently worried about managing change risks at this point, we recommend doing this exercise. If you are sufficiently worried, we can go ahead and move on to our recommended approach.

One of the challenges to managing risks and issues is that many people get confused about which is which. While some people may not realize that this is a problem, it in fact drives a lot of difficulties in the risk/issue management process as the determination of what are risks and what are issues can have an impact on the prioritization of what gets addressed and when. All things being equal, we prioritize the mitigation of issues higher than the mitigation of risks. The reason for that has to do with the differences between the definitions of risks and issues. We recommend utilizing the standard PMBOK definitions:

- A "risk" is something that *could* occur, and has the potential to may negatively impact scope, schedule, quality, and/or cost.

- An "issue" is something that *has* occurred that has the potential to negatively impact, or is negatively impacting scope, schedule, quality, and/or cost.

It is also highly recommended that you be a bit pedantic about making others in your organization stick to these definitions. Again, the amount of energy and focus we put towards managing something may vary depending upon whether it *could* happen or it *has* happened. Properly applying these definitions makes it much easier to make that determination. Impacts being equal, we would of course want to address something that *has* occurred before something that *could* occur.

Definitions aside, the two main activities in the *Journey Management* approach are documenting risks/ issues, and then managing them to eliminate, reduce, or mitigate their negative impact on the project. Just like in the Planning Cycle, our efforts focus on identifying risks/issues of a human capital and change nature that may have been overlooked by the operational project plans. This could include things like communications plans, skill misalignment, launch dates hitting near holidays, or two projects planning to train the sales force during the same month. We also pay particular attention to risks/issues that might impact across projects (see "Coordinating" above). Whenever possible, we should integrate these efforts with the overall program-level risk management approach of your organization. As with many activities we have discussed, if your organization does not take a program-level approach to risk management, the *Journey Management* capability should assume that role.

The most important part of assuming that risk/issue management role is making sure that all the pertinent information is captured in a central repository. There are a wide variety of ways to approach this, and there are even entire software suites (e.g., HP Quality Center or Remedy) that have very robust risk/issue management capabilities. To be honest, however, we don't recommend using of one of those unless the PMO for your organization has already adopted it. They tend to be overbuilt and more focused on IT risk/issues than human capital and change issues. This makes them hard to apply to what we are discussing here. Moreover, they tend to be quite expensive. Most places we work with use something internally developed, like a MS Excel workbook or a MS Access database. Figure 11 illustrates an example of how this can be approached in Excel.

#	Date	Title	Project	Risk/ Issue	Status	Description	Imp. (1 - 5)	Prob. (1 - 5)	Sev. = (I * P)	Description of Impact	Mitigation Status	Due Date	Owner
1	8/11	Success Criteria for PoC	EDW	Risk	Closed	Steve has asked Mark to draft up what it would look like to call the PoC successful. SOW says we're not on the hook for that. Need to determine if it is appropriate for consulting team to take on that	5	0	0	Lack of defined success criteria and may make it difficult to understand when the EDW-F has achieved it goals	Initial success criteria have been defined in the SOW and the EDW-F project charter. Per conversation with Derek on 10/07 Success Criteria are being closed	8/22	Barry
2	2/10	24/7 Support for Off shore resources	R1.1	Risk	New	Delta Inc. may not be set up for 24 hour support	2	5	10	Offshore may be subject to outages.	Mark is currently acting as point of contact on this.		Marc
3	3/9	UAT Testing	R1.0	Risk	Open	There is no slack time in the project plan to allow for slippage in the UAT test effort	5	3	15	Schedule Slippage: There is a risk of Delta Inc. resources not being available for UAT which could result in a slip in the schedule.	Release 1.0 Project Plan and dates distributed to Delta Inc. Program Management (Derek/Albert). Delta Inc. to confirm participation and availability of resources	3/12	Tom
4	3/9	Reporting Repository Incomplete	R1.0	Issue	Open	The Reporting repository sent by legacy vendor is incomplete doesn't contain users/groups etc.	5	5	25	Cannot upload complete repository until full one is received			Marc

Figure 11: Example Risk/Issues Log

While the specific columns in this spreadsheet may vary, there are a few that should always be included. The first is that each risk/issue should have a unique identifier. We usually just number them 1–N in sequential order of when they are entered; this seems to be the simplest approach. That number should follow the entry throughout its life. There should also be identification of the name of the risk, what project it is associated with, whether it is a risk or an issue, its status (e.g., "open" or "closed") and some description of it.

We also recommend having some assessment of the impact of the risk if it occurs and the likelihood of it occurring. The way we usually do this is by assessing each of these on a 1–5 scale, with 1 being the lowest and 5 being the highest. For an issue we would record that as a 5 since it has already occurred. With these two numbers you can simply multiple these two together to get a severity rating. The higher the severity rating, the more attention that item needs. The last bit of information that would be required is some insight on the mitigation plan and status of the actions to execute that plan. There may be other data points that particular organizations would want to capture, but the main thing is making sure that you have all the information required to drive towards your desired performance outcomes.

Driving Towards Defined Performance Outcomes

One of the primary assumptions of *Journey Management* is that change must be strategic. To be strategic, a change must be clearly linked to the specific performance outcomes. This is very similar to the recommendations we find in Balanced Scorecard texts that advocate keeping the organization focused on specific measureable goals that can be measured and managed (Kaplan & Norton, 2001). A key focus of *Journey Management* is promulgating that focus through to the change level.

The first step in this task is developing an understanding of how performance occurs and changes within an organization. There are a variety of ways to approach this, but one of the best we have found is to begin by considering the "performance chain," described in Figure 12.

Influencing factors...	...affect people as they perform tasks...	...that are part of key work processes...	...which enable successful outcomes...	...that achieve business goals.
• Talent Acquisition • Workplace/ Structural • Learning and Development • Managerial and Structural Support • Personal Motivation • Technology	• Identify prospects • Review quality report • Decide on data • Fill out contract • Respond to customer request or email • Open documents	• Sales prospecting • Quality control • Customer Communications • Document preparation	• New customer • Plans • Sales contract • Closed inquiries	• Profits • High returns • Increased profitability • Reduced turnover

Performance occurs in this direction

⟶

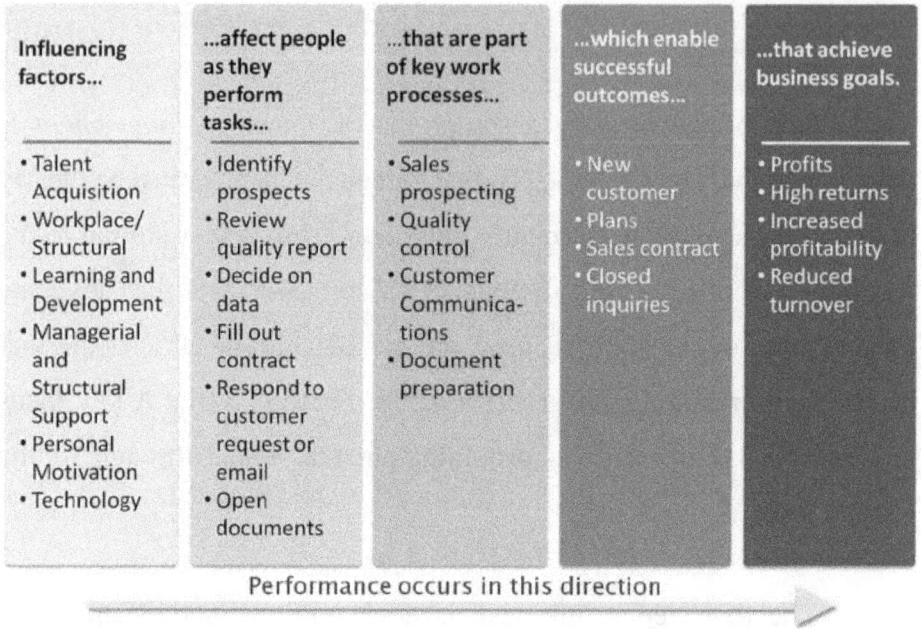

Figure 12: Performance Chain

The performance chain is part of the Performance DNA™ methodology that has also been adopted by the American Society for Training and Development (ASTD). If we examine this graphic from left to right, we will notice that it defines different categories that impact how people perform their jobs. It starts off on the left with tactical influencing factors and moves right towards specific business goals. For any change effort, we must be able to clearly link it to one or more of the categories defined in this graphic. Obviously, the more we can clearly link it, the better.

Establishing this link is important for a variety of reasons, not the least of which is avoiding the sticky situation a client of ours found themselves in many years ago. This particular client was in the housing sector, and the situation occurred back in the early 2000s. Organizations in the housing sector are notoriously late adopters of new technologies. This organization was one of the worst culprits of the bunch. In this case, they had decided to implement an interactive intranet website to manage many of their operational functions that had previously been done manually. It was a fairly robust solution. So robust, in fact, that many people in the organization had hard time using it. One of our contacts there described it as "like putting my 80-year-old great uncle behind the wheel of a Ferrari."

To make matters worse, they had recently been in a meeting with the company's founder and CEO, who, according to rumor, still had his executive assistant print out emails so he could read them and hand-write replies back, which the assistant then typed back to the sender. While this gentleman was extremely busy and not overly focused on this particular effort, he did drop into one status meeting and asked a very important question. That question was "why" they were doing all this. Our client was unable to provide a satisfactory answer to that question. That is when they asked us to get involved.

As you may recall, the late 1990s and early 2000s were a time when many organizations were developing web presences just because it was the thing to do. There was not a lot of consideration for how they helped the organization's strategic goals, or more importantly, how they helped the individuals in that organization achieve their goals. Such was the case here. Luckily, once we started digging down a little bit, we were able to clearly identify the strategic and performance outcomes related to this effort. We were able not only to communicate those to the CEO, but share them with the people in the organization in such a way as to make it clear why this approach helped them meet their jobs easier. More importantly we were able to understand how to measure the outcomes of these efforts.

Measuring the Impacts

It is not enough to passively agree that we want to drive towards some outcome. We must also actively understand what progress we are making towards those goals and have some assessment of our actual (versus planned) progress. This is the logic behind the old saying, "You can't manage what you can't measure." This statement is often attributed to Edward Demming, although several sources dispute that he ever actually said it and attribute the statement to Joseph Juran or other quality experts. Regardless of the actual origin, the idea that we must keep track of our movement towards our goals is valid, and its importance should never be underestimated.

The idea of measuring progress towards a goal is not a new one. Its roots can be traced back to as early as the 19th century, when

Italian economist Vilfredo Pareto began analyzing land ownership and production means (Carey & Lloyd, 1995). Six Sigma was developed at Motorola in the mid 1980s and has since been successfully applied to the manufacturing processes of organizations such as GE and Allied Signal (Pande, Neuman, & Cavanaugh, 2000). One of the most active trends in business today is using analytics to measure this data to create competitive advantage (Davenport & Harris, 2007).

Interestingly, there has not been very much discussion of how to apply measurement to project management—or, more to the point, change management—beyond what is recommended in the PMBOK methodology. The measurements that are recommended in the PMBOK tend to focus on metrics such as percentage complete, estimate to complete, and budget spend. The application of these tends to be more around particular activities being done or not done, rather than how well we are doing. This begs the question: How do we measure how well we are doing with our change efforts towards our business goals?

The simplest way we have found is to go back to the performance chain (Figure 12) and work from right to left rather than from left to right. Starting with the business goals, we determine how we would measure those. Then we cascade to the outcomes and work processes, and do the same activity with special consideration for how to link those to the overall goals. After we have identified the measurements there, we then consider the task activities and influencing factors. For each of those, we identify what metrics we can measure to link those metrics back the overall outcomes we want. This is not unlike the employee-customer-profit chain that was established at Sears many years ago which clearly showed a link between employee satisfaction, customer satisfaction, and profit (Rucci, Kirn, & Quinn, 1998). While the Sears effort involved significant statistical analysis, what we are talking about here does not necessarily need to be that robust. Something as simple as "eye balling" the alignments and using good business judgment will be sufficient.

Another question we often get is how these outcomes should be reported. As with many things related to *Journey Management*, the answer all depends on your organization and what will be most palatable there. For smaller organizations, simple Excel spreadsheets that are updated monthly may do the trick. For larger organizations with more of an analytics appetite, something more robust may be required. We have even seen things as advanced as Business Objects dashboards that pull from large data warehouses that update daily. Keep in mind the reports are intended to inform stakeholder dialogues and decision meetings, so select the report method that will work best for your stakeholders. Figures 13–15 provides an illustration of some of those kinds of reports.

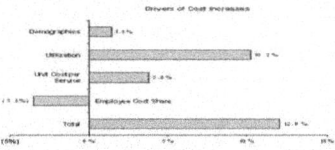

Figure 13: Metrics Example #1

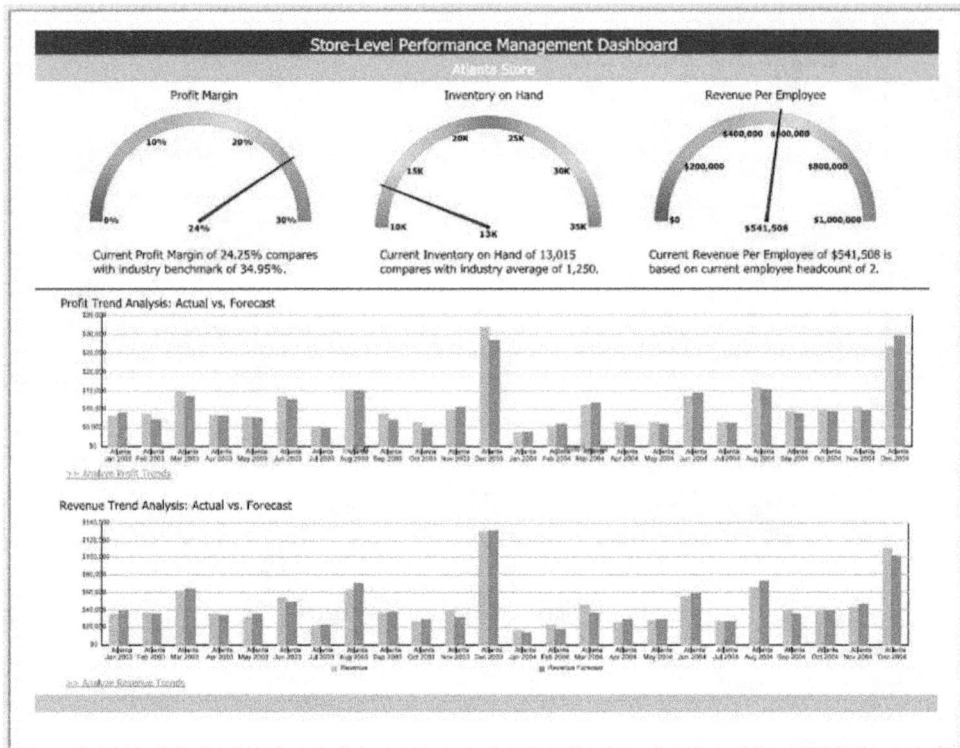

Figure 14: Metrics Example #2

Risk Profile

Group Risk Index	0.66	Chronic Impact	638
Avg Forecasted IP LOS	0.22	Acute Impact	2609
Avg Forecasted ER Visits	0.15	Mover Members	4 %
Avg Forecasted RX Cost	$90	High Risk Members	6 %
# /% Members In Care Mgmt	29 / 0.9 %		

Utilization Profile / **Population Profile**

Admits/1000	45.3	Admits/1000	82.3
Days/1000	150.1	Days/1000	410.6
OP ER Visits/1000	135.4	OP ER Visits/1000	206.2
RX/1000	103.1	RX/1000	8952.6
Avg Total Inpatient Cost	$6,490	Avg Total Paid	$1,903
Avg Professional Cost	$656	Avg Forecasted Cost	$2,484

Guideline Compliance Profile

Guideline Disease	# Members w/Disease	# Non-Compliant Members	Average % Compliance	# Members in Care Management	% Members in Care Management
Asthma	110	110	14 %	0	0 %
CAD	53	53	38 %	1	2 %
CHF	9	9	7 %	3	33 %
COPD	8	8	31 %	1	13 %
CVA	11	11	26 %	1	9 %
Depression	107	105	2 %	2	2 %
Diabetes	70	70	52 %	1	1 %
Hyperlipidemia	367	366	30 %	3	1 %
Preventative Care	2637	893	63 %	29	1 %

Severity Profile

Figure 15: Metrics Example #3

Advanced reports like these not necessarily required, but they do illustrate some of the available options. Many times, the organization already has the right data available; it is just a matter of applying those measurements to the change journey. This goes back to one of our guiding themes for *Journey Management* which is to use what your organization already has wherever possible. While this approach does appeal to CFOs due to reduced cost, the main driver is not so much economics as it is palatability. If the people in the organization are already used to something, stick with that. With the exception of critical capabilities (e.g., the CIM), *Journey Management* is not really the place to be introducing too many revolutionary things when it comes to measurement and reporting. It is probably more productive to take an evolutionary approach.

One thing we do recommend related to the measurement of the change progress that *is* revolutionary, however, is something adapted from Ken Blanchard's *Gung Ho!* (Blanchard & Bowles, 1998). That recommendation is: always cheer the progress. Far too often in business in general—and change in particular—we forget to celebrate accomplishments and achievements. There is somehow this puritanical assumption that people should be satisfied with doing a good job and be happy with that. That is not, however, the case.

As we established early on, change is hard and many people simply do not like it. This statement is not a value judgment on the organization or the people in it; it is simply a fact of corporate life. As such, people need encouragement, pats on the back, and recognition for all their hard work. As a client of ours once said, "They need an occasional $%&#ing happy hour, because they're getting killed on this deal." Measuring the progress gives you something to celebrate. Celebrating gives you momentum. Momentum gives your organization the push it needs to go from one change to the next, to the next—

without getting exhausted. As we established early on, this isn't about one change; it's about the journey.

Conclusion

The focus of this discussion has been how to realize the strategic value of intentionally managing changes and proactively driving business performance goals. We do this by evolving from traditional change management into *Journey Management*. While we have provided clear guidelines, it is important to remember that each journey is unique. Each organization has its own history, culture, and preferences. By integrating your understanding of what makes that organization and its journey unique with the proven framework of our *Journey Management* methodology, we enable organizational leaders to effectively manage through the complexities to achieve the business outcomes needed to succeed. We also develop a change capability that facilitates long-term success. We do this by leveraging our five cycles.

Cycle 1: Awareness

The Awareness Cycle is about getting the people to both recognize and fully internalize that there is a need for the change. At the executive level, it is about understanding the drivers to change and the expected strategic business outcomes when we succeed. If leaders are not aware of the critical need or what good outcomes look like, it is unlikely that they will support the effort. Without leadership's support, the organization will not be fully committed. Changes without full commitment never achieve their business goals.

At the individual level, the Awareness Cycle is about providing people the information they need to understand how the drivers for change and expected outcomes connect to their specific role. This knowledge drives thinking about how work gets done and how people can get that work done better in the context of the strategic goals. Once this train of thought begins, people are more likely to get involved, learn what is expected of them, and ask questions about what is coming next. This is also where we being to gain the commitment of key influencers who can build support in organic and intentional ways.

Cycle 2: Planning

As we discussed, many organizations are pretty good at planning. The problem is that their focus is on the transactional and technical rather than the strategic and human capital. The *Journey Management* Planning Cycle pushes the organization beyond just what gets done, and drives it to also think purposefully about who does what and strategic goals that the change is expected to accomplish.

Planning at the strategic level increases value realization and reduces the chances of unpleasant surprises. It also allows the organization's leaders to clearly recognize the connections between change program plans, observable business outcomes, and strategic goals. This "big picture" context enables executive sponsors to know the implications of decisions not only on the program at hand, but on the interdependent change efforts along the journey.

Along with clear connection to strategic goals, the *Journey Management* Planning Cycle helps ensure that those managing the changes do not lose sight of the necessary human capital needs. Far too many change efforts get derailed halfway through the program because all the resources, decisions, and steering committee time were focused on tactical choices about process and structure with no time or effort for retaining talent, enabling key influencers, or assessing individual readiness. While it is likely that every one of these efforts intends to address these issues, their change models did not specifically focus on the human capital requirements. As a result, they fall off the plans and meeting agendas when time gets short. The unintended outcome is that these important issues are not considered until they become a problem. The *Journey Management* Planning Cycle keeps these issues at the forefront, which makes success much more likely.

Cycle 3: Readiness

It is easy to see why an organization that falls prey to the Field of Dreams Fallacy will not realize its change goals. Yet, so many do so because they don't have an alternative approach to implementing strategic change. The Readiness Cycle takes some of the mystery out of tracking progress on the "people stuff" that most people find too difficult to track or assess. Instead of just training people to use some new tool or process, what we should do is cultivate readiness for all aspects of the change. While details will look different across organizations and functions, cultivating readiness always begins with asking few questions:

- Are people in the organization prepared to take the actions needed to stop current practices and start new ones?
- If not, why not? And what actions do you need to take so they are ready?
- If yes, what actions do you need to take to ensure they stay on-track through to benefits realization?

If we can answer "yes, we are ready," we know that our human capital progress and our program progress are in sync. If the answer is "no, we are not ready," we have to take clear and proactive action to move ourselves in that direction. Once we do that and lay a strong foundation for success, we can then begin coordinating the efforts and taking the needed actions.

Cycle 4: Coordinating

Any organization of a reasonable size will have multiple changes going on at any given time. While it can be challenging enough to manage one significant change, like an ERP implementation, imagine coordinating an ERP implementation across multiple European markets while restructuring a global business at the same time. Traditional change management approaches are not sufficient for coordinating these efforts and helping executives make informed choices about how the programs support the strategic goals.

It is not unusual for the decisions related to one change project to have the potential to impact another project. Far too often, however, no one realizes it until months later when they hit a roadblock. By then, it is an expensive and difficult fix. This could all be avoided, however, if the executive sponsors and other decision-making stakeholders had the right information in an easy-to-use format to inform their choices and clarify the implications. The Change Integration Map (CIM) we introduced provides a format to display an intuitive representation of the complex interdependencies that come into play when coordinating multiple change projects. Using such an approach should give everyone involved the right information to make good decisions across the enterprise.

Cycle 5: Executing

Most experienced project managers will say they are very comfortable within the Executing Cycle of *Journey Management*. On the surface it feels like familiar territory. That is intentional, because an important part of the Executing Cycle is being in sync with traditional project management methodologies, such as PMBOK. The challenge, however, is that this comfort can also be risky because there are a couple of key distinctions between the *Journey Management* Execution Cycle and what we find in classic change management and project management. If we overlook the nuances of those distinctions, the full benefit of the *Journey Management* approach may not be realized.

The first distinction relates to how we surface and manage risks and issues. Traditional change management doesn't always consider risks and issues. Most project management methodologies focus primarily on technology and operational risks and issues. Our approach extends that focus to incorporate strategic outcomes and the human capital risks and issues. This more holistic approach allows us to surface more information, highlight more interdependencies, and identify risks and issues that might normally have been overlooked. It is important to note that the management and mitigation of these types of risks and issues often requires more runway than do technical and operational risks. They can also have a more lasting impact when not addressed. As such, a *Journey Management* approach that escalates them early can have a big impact on success.

The second distinction is how our approach links execution efforts to performance outcomes. Traditional change management and project management execution efforts are focused just on the project itself. Most of the evaluative efforts are measures of things like schedule and budget variance. There is almost an assumption that completing the project on time and on budget (or at least somewhere close to that) will result in better performance for the organization and the people in it. The *Journey Management* Execution Cycle does not make such a dangerous assumption. In fact, it forces us to ask how each outcome of the change will positively impact the organization in the people in it. If we can't answer that question, we then need to reevaluate how and/or why we are pursuing this effort. Asking these questions is the difference between managing deliverables and tactics, versus managing performance. Only by managing performance outcomes can we achieve true value realization.

By applying these cycles we can expand beyond the siloed and purely tactical approaches to change and project management, and instead leverage a robust while easy-to-understand approach that informs choices and surfaces issues and opportunities across entire organizations. For example, if we are creating two-way communication channels across our global organization to get people ready for the new CEO, why not use the same channels to create readiness for the new R&D business process and the new self-service HR system? Too many organizations use inconsistent methods for reaching the same people about different programs, without connecting the dots. Why not take a more integrated and coordinated approach?

The choice to leverage the more synchronized approach seems obvious, but there are far too many examples of organizations where the stakeholders never even knew that the same employees were being asked for input by three different projects at the same time. They would only find out when people complained about uncoordinated projects wasting their time resources. *Journey Management* ensures a consistent focus on coordinating across those projects so that you can achieve your strategic business goals in a more synergistic and logical way.

Most importantly, *Journey Management* instills the organizational habits that increase our capacity to effectively deliver programs and projects. Developing these habits builds the internal capability to "change well" and "change fast," which gives us a strategic advantage over competitors who are still stuck with the old way of doing business. If we integrate *Journey Management* into our organizations we create "strategic benefits squared" rather than "trouble squared." And that is a change worth doing.

Works Cited

Blanchard, K., & Bowles, S. (1998). *Gung Ho! Turn On the People in Any Organization.* New York, NY: William Morrow & Company.

Burke, W. W. (2002). *Organizational Change: Theory and Practice.* Thousand Oaks, CA: SAGE Publications.

Carey, R. G., & Lloyd, R. C. (1995). *Measuring Quality Improvement in Healthcare: A Guide to Statistical Process Control Applications.* Milwaukee, WI: American Society for Quality.

Cooperrider, D. L., Sorensen, P. F., Yaeger, T. F., & Whitney, D. (2005). *Appreciative Inquiry: Foundations in Positive Organization Development.* Champaign, IL: Stipes Publishing, LLC.

Covey, S. R. (2004). *The 7 Habits of Highly Effective People: Powerful Lessons in Personal Change.* New York, NY: Free Press.

Davenport, T. H., & Harris, J. G. (2007). *Competing on Analytics: The New Science of Winning.* Boston, MA: Harvard Business School Press.

Gladwell, M. (2002). *The Tipping Point: How Little Things Can Make a Big Difference.* Boston, MA: Little Brown and Company.

Kaplan, R. S., & Norton, D. P. (2004). *Strategy Maps: Converting Intangible Assets into Tangible Outcomes.* Boston, MA: Harvard Business School.

Kaplan, R. S., & Norton, D. P. (2001). *The Strategy Focused Organization: How Balanced Scorecard Companies Thrive in the New Business Environment.* Boston, MA: Harvard Business School Press.

Kelman, H. C. (1958). Compliance, Identification, and Internalization: Three Processes of Attitude Change. *Conflict Resolution*, II(I), 51–60.

Meinert, D. (2012). Wings of Change. *HR Magazine* , 30–36.

Pande, P. S., Neuman, R. P., & Cavanaugh, R. R. (2000). *The Six Sigma Way: How GE, Motorola, and Other Top Companies are Honing Their Performance.* New York, NY: McGraw-Hill.

Rucci, A. J., Kirn, S. P., & Quinn, R. T. (1998). The Employee-Customer-Profit Chain at Sears. *Harvard Business Review* , 76, 82-97.

Schein, E. H. (2003). *DEC is Dead, Long Live DEC.* San Francisco: Berrett-Koehler Publishers Inc.

Stych, E. (2012, February 14). *Feds: Delta Air Lines' Customer Service Improved in 2011.*" Retrieved from http://www.bizjournals.com/twincities/news/2012/02/14/delta-customer-service-improves.html

Worley, C. G., Hitchin, D. E., & Ross, W. R. (1996). *Integrated Strategic Change: How Organizational Development Builds Competitive Advantage.* Reading, MA: Addison-Wesley Publishing Company.

List of Figures

About the Authors

Jimmy Brown, Ph.D.

Jimmy Brown, Ph.D., is a senior consulting executive with 18 years experience delivering practical strategies for business performance improvement. Prior to founding the J. Brown Group, Dr. Brown held senior-level consulting positions at marquee firms such as Booz Allen Hamilton, Accenture, and Hewlett-Packard. In these roles, Dr. Brown has worked across several industries sectors including healthcare (provider, payer, and bio-pharma), retail, high-tech, manufacturing, energy and Federal government (civilian and DoD). He is regularly sought out for his insights on how to apply cutting-edge theory to solve real-world business challenges.

Dr. Brown received his Master's Degree in Industrial and Organizational Psychology from the University of Tulsa, and his Ph.D. from Benedictine University's award-winning organizational development program. In addition to his consulting work, he is a professor in several graduate psychology and management programs.

He can be contacted through www.jbrowngroup.com or his personal website at www.jimmybrownphd.com.

Jill Royston

Jill Royston works at the intersection of individual choice and organizational performance. An Executive Coach and Senior Management Consultant, she brings over 15 years of experience developing people and organizations to improve business performance. Clients rely on Ms. Royston to unlock the potential in leaders and emerging talent, to achieve business goals through intentional organizational design and process improvement, and to live business strategy by successfully implementing change programs that result in new ways of working. Ms. Royston has held internal and external consulting positions working across a spectrum of clients, ranging from complex global organizations to mid-sized US-based businesses and start-ups. She is currently a Principal Consultant with Beacon Associates.

A lifelong learner and mentor, Ms. Royston holds a Master's in Organization Development from American University and a Bachelor's in English from the University of Maryland, Baltimore County. She is affiliated with the Center for Human Systems practitioner's program and was a founding member of the Organization Development Master's Program at the University of Delaware, Lerner School of Business.

Jill can be reached at jroyston@beaconassociates.net

Notes

[1] Project Management Institute Website

http://www.pmi.org/

[2] MS Excel Project Plan Examples

http://office.microsoft.com/en-us/templates/simple-project-plan-TC103345704.aspx

http://www.makeuseof.com/tag/excel-project-management-tracking-templates/

[3] Set up MS Project Baseline
http://office.microsoft.com/en-us/project-help/create-or-update-a-baseline-or-an-interim-plan-HA010156784.aspx

[4] Cat Herding Video

http://www.youtube.com/watch?v=m_MaJDK3VNE

www.ingramcontent.com/pod-product-compliance
Lightning Source LLC
Chambersburg PA
CBHW032008190326
41520CB00007B/396